homopup

queer dog poetry

edited by gerry gomez pearlberg

CLEIS
PRESS

Published in the United States by Cleis Press Inc., P.O. Box 14697, San Francisco, California 94114.

Printed in the United States.
Cover and text design: Scott Idleman / Blink
Cover photo: American Images Inc
Logo art: Juana Alicia
10 9 8 7 6 5 4 3 2 1

Library of Congress Cataloging-in-Publication Data

Homopup: queer dog poetry / edited by Gerry Gomez Pearlberg
      p.   cm.
    ISBN 1-57344-071-X (pbk.)
    1. Dogs–Poetry. 2. Gays' writings, American. 3. American
poetry–20th century. 4. Dog owners–United States–Poetry.
I. Pearlberg, Gerry.
PS595.D63Q44   2008
811' .50803629722'08664–dc21

Acknowledgments

A number of dogstargirls and boys indulged this fantasy of mine and helped to make it real. First and foremost, Frédérique Delacoste and Felice Newman, my publishers, who appreciated the concept and brought it to life. I am extremely grateful to them both, not only for wanting to publish this book, but for ushering it through the process with such enthusiastic care and attention.

For help along the way in locating poems and poets, spreading the word and supporting the effort, I would like to thank Nancy Boutilier, Angie Estes, Scott Hightower, Keith Kahla, Frances Kunreuther, Michael Lassell, Jed Mattes, Esther Newton, Roz Parr, David Trinidad and Alina Troyano.

Jumbo dog biscuits in great abundance to Tristan Taormino for all she did to help make this happen. And to Joan Larkin for being a great pal as well as a great editor.

To dogstargirls and dogstarboys
everywhere, and to our dogs.

And for Otto.

Contents

To Sally
Happy
Birthday
2014

Introduction

O golden mountain, yellow as a beagle's eye!
— *Frank O'Hara*

The reasons for this poetry collection are—like dogs themselves—earnest and unadorned: this was a book I wanted on my shelf, a book I wanted to read to my dog, a book I hoped others would enjoy.

The inspiration for a collection of dog poems by lesbian and gay poets occurred in 1994, while I was editing an anthology of lesbian love poems called *The Key to Everything*, a project that gave me the perfect excuse—in fact required me—to gluttonously consume every lesbian poetry publication I could get my hands on. While searching for love poetry, I encountered poem after poem in which the presence of dogs was deeply felt. The first was Judith's McDaniel's devastating "Dangerous Memory," followed by Chrystos' raunchy "On the Phone," Eloise Klein Healy's "Moon on the Porch," Terry Wolverton's "Requiem," Elizabeth Bishop's "Pink Dog," and others by Gertrude Stein, May Swenson, Jan Freeman, Linda Smukler, Eileen Myles and Melinda Goodman. For my own pleasure, I created a small file folder of these poems—the genesis of *Queer Dog: Homo/Pup/Poetry.*

A bloodhound at heart, I soon initiated a full-scale dog-hunt through the many books by gay male poets that graced my shelves, and discovered wonderful offerings by Langston Hughes, James Schuyler, Mark Doty, Michael Klein, Richard Harteis, Dennis Cooper, Thom Gunn and W. H. Auden. I sent out a call for submissions inviting lesbian, gay and bisexual poets to send dog-related or dog-focused poems that in one way or another "shed" light on the intersections between canine culture and queer sensibility. I sought poems that were, like dogs themselves, serious, goofy, tender, vicious, sexy, rabid, and raw. In response I received work from well over one hundred poets (including several self-identified "cat people"), many of whom are represented here. Fellow poets brought a few more indispensable strays to my attention, and the pack was formed.

Dogs run through every one of these poems, just as, one might argue, the very essence of poetry runs through dogs. Poetry and dogs share a number of qualities—they're both immediate, temporal, social creatures; they are souls laid bare for all the world to see, yet full of hidden implication. In any good poem, there's an invisible shade of energy, thought and emotion that lies beyond the grasp of language. I like to think of that as the same realm where dogs come by their unique powers, their sense of thrill and hunt and humor, their gentle devotion.

That said, it should be clear that a book of queer poems about dogs, plain and simple, would be just dandy, but of course the work you'll encounter in these pages involves a great deal more than that. These poems, which range from elegy to light verse, cast their gaze on whole universes of experiences and ideas. They are about love and love lost, about mortality and the impact of AIDS. They are about queer (and canine) rituals of courtship, sexuality and sexual liberation. They are about the interior arena of spirit, the nature of art and life, and—yes—the meaning of "family." They are about betrayal and infidelity, consciousness and conscience. They are about Greyhounds, Bulldogs, Airedales, Poodles and puppies of all denominations.

Why do gay men and lesbians have so much to say on the subject of dogs? Perhaps because we're masters at reconfiguring what it means to create family, what it means to be animal and living in skin, what it means to exist in a state of exuberant, unapologetic disobedience. Perhaps it's because dogs, like queers, are in your face; they speak their minds and are themselves, utterly and precisely. It's probably also got something to do with our appreciation of great company, our love of a good time, and our tendency to form nontraditional interpersonal bonds and emotional attachments. Or maybe it has something to do with the "sense of theatre" that W.H. Auden attributes to our four-legged friends in "Talking to Dogs" and the gift for re-imagining the underpinnings of identity that Gertrude Stein seems to have presaged in "Identity A Poem."

Whatever the reason, the evidence of queer interest—and queer *poetic* interest—in the subject of dogs is here before you to enjoy. Read it to your pup tonight.

Gerry Gomez Pearlberg

Fifi, the dangerous fag dog
John Del Peschio

Fifi, the dangerous fag dog,
makes guys nervous,
gay or straight.
She's so femme!
Pink ribboned,
she knows
drag queens' stones
were Stonewall's first stones.
She knows mincing gaits got there.
Fifi, strut,
you feisty bitch,
strut your dangerous rhinestones.

Sign
Linda Smukler

I forgot to tell you about the red sheets my sister bought for us that were incredibly cheap on sale and that we couldn't replace with the blue sheets we wanted because the blue sheets were now full price   I forgot to tell you about the reason I wanted to make love last night and instead we had a fight I forgot to tell you that I came out in sign class   a class of twenty or so under-thirty women and one man all from the teaching professions   all straight from E. Greenbush   I forgot to tell you that the week before the teacher asked me do you have children and I snapped my fingers together to say no and slapped my hip to say I had a dog   she made me finger spell our dog's name and then the teacher said bring pictures of your family next week   I forgot to tell you that this week I brought pictures of you and our dog   I showed them to the class and when asked I slapped my hip and gave the sign for dog and pointed to the picture of you and made the sign for love and person which is the sign for love person or lover and some of the students looked at me and were very polite some even smiled   it was so easy to say husband and children and all I wanted to say was lover and dog so I wondered why after all these years I still had to blush

Dogged Love
Jack Anderson

It all began
when Jeff
(who lived around the corner)
and Ray
(who didn't know him then,
but lived around the other corner)
decided to get dogs,
and for the same reason:

dog-walking, both thought,
could be a form of cruising,
a dog could be
a fit topic of conversation
for any nice stranger
who wanted to meet them,
but didn't know what to say.

Jeff got Wagstaff
and Ray got Beau,
and one night they met
(Jeff and Ray,
Wagstaff and Beau)
and found they lived
just around the corner.

It was love at first sight
—Jeff and Ray,

Wagstaff and Beau—
and soon they moved in
with one another,
and they all lived happily—
but not ever after:

Jeff and Ray quarreled,
then they quarreled some more
and spoke of moving out,
yet didn't,

for Wagstaff and Beau
were as happy as ever,
and any time someone
even mentioned moving
they'd stare with sad
accusing eyes
and whimper and moan.

So that's how it is,
they're still where they were,
though Jeff and Ray
are perpetually snappish
and seldom speak,
except to growl;
yet they've made their sacrifice
for the sake of true love

so Wagstaff and Beau
can stay together,
barking ecstatically
all day and all night.

Moon on the Porch
Eloise Klein Healy

Moon on the porch thumps his tail when I climb
the stairs. He's got a rock in his mouth, old dog,
and will I play? Old teeth worn into stubs
from carrying rocks. Old Moon who limps
as far as we'll walk him. Drinks from the hot
tub when you're not looking, when the moon slides
over the edge of the roof and naked into the water.
I didn't know then this would be a poem to all
my lovers, planted by you in the full moon,
the water running off your breasts, falling
like silver coins into a pool. I didn't know then
how many women I was learning to love.

Oriane
James Schuyler

My name is Oriane,
the lurcher:
half whippet, half border collie,
bred to course
for hares and rabbits
(there are no hares,
only rabbits):
and so I do,
and chase my rubber ball
and play in waves,
and cuddle
in arms that love me.
This is my home:
its name is
                    Oriane

from *Paris France*
Gertrude Stein

The French like to call beasts up-to-date names, names of people do not change much but they like to follow the fashion in animals' names.

It always pleases me that French boys are often called Jean-Marie, you can use a female name to go with a man's name, it hallows the male name to add the female name to it, and that is civilised and logical and might be fashionable, it has always existed.

But the animals' names are a different matter, there are all the regular names and then there are other ones. I remember the pleasure in hearing a farmer call one of his oxen Landru, is it really his name I asked oh yes, he said, but not because he is a murderer, oh no, he said, just to like it. Of course most female dogs are called Diane, that is inevitable, but all the terriers have English names, they are called Jimmie and Tom and one is known as Nicky Boy de Belley.

Our dog's name is Basket and the French like that, it sounds well in French and goes very well with Monsieur, the children all call him Monsieur Basket more or less to rhyme with casquette.

That was the first Basket.

We did love the first Basket and he was shaved like a real poodle and he did fait le beau and could say how do you do and he was ten years old and last autumn just after our return to Paris he died. We did cry and cry and finally every one said get another dog and get it right away.

Henry Daniel-Rops said get another as like Basket as possible call him by the same name and gradually there will be confusion and you will not know which Basket it is. They had done that twice with their little white Teneriffe which they call Claudine.

And then I saw Picasso, and he said no, never get the same kind of a dog again never, he said I tried it once and it was awful, the new one reminded me of the old one and the more he looked like him the worse it was. Why said he, supposing I were to die, you would go out on the street and sooner or later you would meet a Pablo, but it would not be I and it would be the same. No never get the same kind of a dog, get an Afghan hound, he has one, and Jean Hugo had said I could have one, but they are so sad, I said, that's all right for a Spaniard, but I don't like dogs to be sad, well he said get what you like but not the same, and as I went out he repeated not the same no not the same.

So we tried to have the same and not to have the same and there was a very large white poodle offered to us who looked like a young calf with black spots and other very unpleasant puppies with little pink eyes and then at last we found another Basket, and we got him and we called him Basket and he is very gay and I cannot say that the confusion between the old and the new has yet taken place but certainly le roi est mort vive le roi, is a normal attitude of mind.

I was a little worried what Picasso would say when he saw the new Basket who was so like the old Basket but fortunately the new Basket does stand on his legs in some indefinable way a little the way an Afghan hound stands on his although Basket the new Basket is pure poodle, and I pointed this out to Picasso when we and our dogs met on the street and that did rather reconcile him to it.

It is rather interesting that the Frenchman said have the same and the Spaniard said no don't have the same. The Frenchman does realise the inevitability of le roi est mort vive le roi but the Spaniard does not recognise the inevitability of resemblances and continuation. He just does not but a Frenchman just does.

And now this Basket being a war-dog, that is living in the country with us all the time in war-time is very much a village dog and although the village spends a great deal of time discussing whether he is more or less beautiful than the last one, whether he is bigger and whether he is more affectionate the children like him but they treat him with less respect, they call him Basket familiarly they do not call him Monsieur Basket, there is that difference in their character, I mean the character of this Basket and that Basket. But for all that he is a very sweet Basket, any dog one loves is a very sweet dog and poor Madame Pierlot has just lost her Jimmie, and he was just the same age as the other Basket.

Yoko
Thom Gunn

All today I lie in the bottom of the wardrobe
feeling low but sometimes getting up
to moodily lumber across rooms
and lap from the toilet bowl, it is so sultry
and then I hear the noise of firecrackers again
all New York is jaggedy with firecrackers today
and I go back to the wardrobe gloomy
trying to void my mind of them.
I am confused, I feel loose and unfitted.

At last deep in the stairwell I hear a tread,
it is him, my leader, my love.
I run to the door and listen to his approach.
Now I can smell him, what a good man he is,
I love it when he has the sweat of work on him,
as he enters I yodel with happiness,
I throw my body up against his, I try to lick his lips,
I care about him more than anything.

After we eat we go for a walk to the piers.
I leap into the standing warmth, I plunge into
the combination of old and new smells.
Here on a garbage can at the bottom, so interesting,
what sister or brother I wonder left this message I sniff.
I too piss there, and go on.
Here a hydrant there a pole
here's a smell I left yesterday, well that's disappointing

but I piss there anyway, and go on.

I investigate so much that in the end
it is for form's sake only, only a drop comes out.

I investigate tar and rotten sandwiches, everything, and go on.

And here a dried old turd, so interesting
so old, so dry, yet so subtle and mellow.
I can place it finely, I really appreciate it,
a gold distant smell like packed autumn leaves in winter
reminding me how what is rich and fierce when excreted
becomes weathered and mild
                                              but always interesting
and reminding me of what I have to do.

My leader looks on and expresses his approval.

I sniff it well and later I sniff the air well
a wind is meeting us after the close July day
rain is getting near too but first the wind.

Joy, joy,
being outside with you, active, investigating it all,
with bowels emptied, feeling your approval
and then running on, the big fleet Yoko,
my body in its excellent black coat never lets me down,
returning to you (as I always will, you know that)
and now
            filling myself out with myself, no longer confused,
my panting pushing apart my black lips, but unmoving,
I stand with you braced against the wind.

The Grace of Animals
Richard Harteis

I.

Long before the adult flora of
sex, ambition, and money overgrew
the moral landscape, I recall thinking
I might possibly not be able to believe
in a God who denied a place in heaven
for animals, in particular my blue terrier
who was the single friend of my lonely boyhood.

II.

I could see their lesser intelligence, I
was reading about dinosaurs then and Darwin
like other boys, even aspiring to Aquinas.
But I couldn't accept that something so
beautiful, something which responded so
completely to my being would become
dumb earth while I, my brothers and sisters,
and Sister Marguerite would, would what?
buzz eternal in a perfect inanimate rapture,
paradise, glowing Godhead?

Couldn't there be an antechamber, a
little limbo say, some way for Astra
to live with me after death since

till then she was the only star in my life?
I began to read Egyptian theology which
seemed closer to how things ought to be.

III.

The good guest recently, I walked
with my host's child and his dog
while the adults drank
night caps and did dishes:
"Feel her, feel her," he said,
unselfconscious in the delight of
her satin coat, a little afraid the
black lab might knock him down again
going for a squirrel, but determined
with his entire small weight (half the dog's)
and soul to try to train this gentle monster,
who had a pretty good idea how to train this boy.

IV.

Ten years ago for my mother's birthday I
bought a scottie puppy. With pointed
ears and little skirt it was a cookie
cutter version of Franklin Roosevelt's pet.
The dog lived her quiet secret scottie life
all these years, the black eyes, black coals
at the far end of her face structure, hidden
in the bushy eyebrows—the kind of success
one hopes for in life, giving a good gift.

V.

This morning, insomniac and firm,
mother calls from retirement and Florida
to declare I must put the dog to sleep.
The pet has become incontinent, a burden to
relatives, snaps at the children occasionally
and is too much an expense.

This woman is as good as Simone de Beauvoir
or Saint Teresa, no irony is lost on her.
It's what has kept her awake all night I suppose,
this coming to the end and telling me firmly
how to deal with age, and loneliness and death
the way earlier she taught me how to deal with
youth and loneliness and life.

Now mother returns the gift, gives me
the chance to comfort, to say, "No,
I understand, but I think I'll try her here,
see if she can be happy here, no need to
put her to sleep yet. You have made your
decision, don't worry, I accept the responsibility
and it's not a burden."

And it is clearer than ever
how if there is a God
he gives us these creatures
to lead us here and there.

Dog Days
Michael Klein

Franz Schubert, in this life, is six weeks old in the body
of a chocolate-brown labrador who reminds me that risk
is extra life when he takes my hand easily in his
mouth and leads me through new teeth and a snowfall blanking town.
I think this snow must be able to lift two children, who
are fighting, out of their argumentative skins and make

a day so bright, it winces. What is ever this willing?
This vibrant dog with me, loving my hand as if it could
delay his life a little, makes me want to be him and
his newborn smile: play-ferocious on the way to heartbreak.
Reaching it back to the perfect wet arc of young bone that
forces itself into the roof of Franz's mouth, my hand

follows with my body and enters him. It is summer
again in the canoes. The man I come to when he calls,
approaches, first on a wrinkle of water, then as
himself, and we are ready to go. Franz, good dog, inside
me this is life I did not choose and you have yours, ready.

The Other Language

Timothy Liu

Nothing on the pages
can articulate what we did
not trust. Last night, a dog
with your face spoke to me.
My eyes were closed,
the heavy balls of dreams
sliding back and forth
in their separate cells
like synchronized swimmers,
each tacit movement a gift
we did not share, that dog
talking in a language
that does not belong to us.

Mountain Rhyme
Jan Freeman

Sorrow placed its tongue on my thigh.
Open up, Sorrow said, let me in.
Turntables swung the lyrics aside.
Little flower, they sang, *mein kind.*

She cuddles the dog and she coddles the dog.
She says she's in love, now, with the dog;
and I follow on walks or watch their eyes
as they tenderly touch what I once touched.

Let me in, said Sorrow. You're in, I said,
you're up to my neck, you're near my head;
you've filled my belly with a tear of lead.
It's good to be home, Sorrow said.

the same dogs
Ana Marie Castañon

in the path of my headlights
entering the freeway on-ramp two shadows
something two dogs about to wander into traffic
going to get killed wearing worn out expressions
helpless soaked from the hard rain
i pull over quickly trying not to hit them
turn on my yellow flashers get out cautiously
they stand still for me
as i reach for their desperate collars
they let me pick them up
this little one goes in the car eagerly
right for the front seat to wait
and watches me struggle with the larger one
i can barely heave him
reluctantly into the back
i get inside try to read their tags
they slobber on my hands nuzzle my neck
and now we are all going somewhere
i picture them living in my small backyard
snowy the little white one
and jesse medium-sized brown like me
on a ride to safety in bleakest weather
we drive for miles to find a gas station
where the phone booth is lit
call the number on the tags
ask the man answering if he knows a dog named snowy

and a brown dog he wants to know how they got so far away
we wait in my car steaming up windows
wet and soggy shaking off water everywhere
looking into dark brown eyes that say who are you
panting it feels good with you here
we pet each other with dirty paws
whimpering what's gonna happen now
in half an hour the people come looking for us
i have to let jesse and snowy out they hesitate
and seem unsure about climbing into the back of a jeep
that belongs to some middle-aged men
jesse watches me through the rear window
as they drive away again toward the freeway on-ramp
i follow close behind he keeps staring at me
wondering where i am going maybe
why i don't turn on my headlights
i finally realize they are off
even in this dim slushy rain the car
steers blindly feels empty already slow on my way
wanting jesse and snowy to keep me
take me home lick my face stay with me
until my quiet howling is over we are the same dogs
lost and needing to be rescued

New Poem
Eileen Myles

My lover came over my house
one afternoon—I was doing
a big mailing for a show—
the one before this. She
was crying and I was trying
to make her happy. I was
sitting on the floor in this
sand chair we bought to go
camping last summer. I
was sitting there counting all
the people in the zip code
one thousand three. Myra
announced she was leaving
and I started to do a
little dance from my
chair—I was making
faces and had paws
it was a little dog dance
I explained to her. It's
a little dog chorus line.
A show about a chorus
line of dogs. But dog
chorus lines are irregular.
They just wander all over
the city, stray dogs.

Related but not you
know doing anything in
sync, but shitting eating
pissing fucking   just having
a dog life. That kind
of chorus. It's a
very modern art, the
dog chorus line and
I thought about all
the dogs on my lap I was
mailing my postcards to.
Eventually we got sick of
the shape of that kind
of dog chorus line. It
was true, but there's
so much of that, truth,
and it's so irregular so
we decided to make something
new—dogs in saddles,
dogs sprayed blue &
gilded, you know arranged
in galleries or groupings.
The irony of that kind
of product, an external
order, that's the joke,
despite the fact the
dogs are still roaming
around hungry &
hopeless, we're getting
very involved with

the new blue dogs
God, now we can decorate
them so many different
ways and we feel
so hopeless about
life, what can we
really do, so we
find another funny
way to arrange the
dogs, make a big
show, act as if
just for a second you
can have some kind of control,
and it is kind of funny, I
mean dogs aren't blue

Pet Names
Bernard Cooper

Go ahead. Call me Zacko, Hound Thing, Gray Beard.
Rug Thumper, Fur Face, Curlicue, Nose Head.
Goof Bear, Smudge Pot, Fuzz Bucket, Sonny.

His Dogness, Pasha, Doodle, Black Lips.
Wolf Bane, Mister, Creature, Minky.
Barker, Bone Boy, Will O' the Whisker.

Doggy-Come-Lately, Nanook-of-the-Hearth.
Rutter, Pisser, Sniffer-at-Air.
Chaser-of-Tail, He-Who-Licks-Floor.

I go by none of these names. And more.

—Zachary

Gay Dog
Mark Bibbins

I saw it one day as I was walking by,
displayed in an obscure sun-bleached corner of
the window of an adult video store
on Eighth Avenue.

Light and time had worked together to nearly
obliterate the sordid images on
the cardboard boxes showing the usual
array of nude forms,

but the most decidedly *un*usual
may also be had by the more intrepid
connoisseurs of pornographic videos
who frequent the store.

The video of which I speak is called *Gay
Dog.* Its title character is a German
Shepherd with a predilection for licking
his master's penis,

as the cover photograph would indicate.
To help the canine get into character,
the aforementioned member looks like it is
covered with chocolate

pudding. (This particular actor belongs
to both the obedience *and* method schools.)
It seems rather unfair to deceive man's best
friend in such a way.

That this would have an audience speaks volumes
about our own species; being no stranger
to the tricks which some men will employ just to
have someone lick them,

I can empathize with this fellating pooch.
Now, let us raise the stakes, and, in so doing,
vindicate our animal friends. I propose
a sequel to this

questionable movie, one which I would most
gladly be among the first in line to buy.
I have already devised the plot and a
fine title: *Gay Shark.*

Foo Dog Blues

Tim Dlugos

So many dynasties, so little time:
the slogan on a T-shirt I could buy
in Heaven, if someone in a uniform
would spell me from my duties at the gate.
Heaven's a boutique out here, like Greetings,
Design Observations, and All American
Boy back home, a member of the nouveau
mercantile class: shops that sound
like elements of waking life, posture,
form and aspiration. Meanwhile, cousins
Fortitude and Patience languish where the steel
bands play calypso music and the dope
smoke wafts through rotting incunabula.
I'm glad that my commission is divine,
albeit impossible. It makes the borders
clear, sets my cap and large incisors
on edge, cutting through the day's detritus,
the piling up of detail in a wooly rug
I wear around my neck like the lion
I was: an ancient teacher's cub scout,
trained to watch and wait with eager paw
clutching a small pearl atop a silken
pillow, a ladies' magazine's idea of grit
and purpose, the synthesis of price and pride.
Atlantic and Pacific, they know the terrific

power of the sentry, and his burden.
I've been around for years, and am almost
invisible, like the guardian angels. A ring
of fire is how they first appeared, worlds away from
the consumptive blondes with pastel bathrobes
and wings who populate the wayside chapel
windows: a down-to-earth caricature of life
unknown among the sensible, the purely
spiritual being. When gods come down
to earth they appear as nondescript travelers
whose every gesture is a test. Sit awhile
and stroke my mane beneath this banyan. Babe
the Blue Ox strolls by, lowing for his patron,
exemplar of the brawn that built this country,
strange as that may seem. I meander
over to the bridge, and nuzzle Marco Polo
as he stares into the river, surrounded by dogs.
He's something never seen before in these parts.
In the water, he can see the goldfish dart
beneath the stones, and on the muddy bank
rabbits with the fungus of longevity
between their paws, under a full moon.
They nibble when they eat. And I've outlived them
all, fierce as ever, though I've put a groove
in my paw where the pearl fits: can't lose that.
The halcyon days of puppyhood with sticks
of incense in my mouth, the smoke ribbons
curling like a halo—good dog!—around my ears;
all the years of smiling or sneering, they never

knew which; and now the humdrum stream
of traffic past the phony oriental
gates, palm trees on the dusty street,
rumble of the good earth far below. Tarzana
is a far cry from nirvana, and for an illusion,
maya stings. I've never caught a rabbit;
that's not my job. And you're right, I've never
been a friend of yours. I have been selected
for a special task, a destiny unique in history.
To the impious, it sounds like a Disney
short: The Cat Who Thought He Was A Dog.
But for robbers, and floods, and fires, and even
the eventual earthquake, I mean business:
a guardian set in stone by a forgotten artist
commissioned by the emperor who brought us floods
and fires and the eventual earthquake.
He wanted the moon, and tried to reach it
via firecracker; you probably have heard the rest.
I want to close my mouth and rest with the moon
in my face, facing a stream of travelers
who pass me single file on their way to the interior
and touch me as they pass, for good luck;
and join the other dogs, the real ones,
on the explorer's bridge waiting for the stranger
for whom the mundane happenings of these parts
are a great adventure, something to drive him on.

Power Source
Edward Field

Like harnessing
the tides or the wind,
how about attaching
dogs' tails
to power generators?

I want the job
of patting the dog
to keep its tail
wagging.

Dogs could generate
enough electricity
for cities, for countries—
light up the world!

Barking Sands
Eva Yaa Asantewaa

Wind barks. Sun bites. Cliffs glower. Yet, on Kauaian sands, two gold-brown dogs are mellow today. Waves swallow their gold-brown surfer boys in rippling silver.

Tallulah finds her stick, trots up to a princess walking the shore. "She looks like a smart girl," Tallulah thinks, tail fluttering. "Here, throw this stick for me. We'll make a game of it, and the day will go."

Marlena turns her noble head into the mist, searching the sea foam as white as egrets in the canebrake. "Where *are* those boys?" she thinks. She whispers, "Wild sky orchids, feathery clouds…oh, luscious day, stay here with me. Do not go."

The stick arcs high. Tallulah's muscles fire, and she flies. Marlena waits.

Barking Sands, named for the sound of the wind, is a beach on the western coast of the Hawaiian island of Kauai.

Strong Light Behind You
Fran Winant

Strong light behind you
shines right through your ears
and through thin membranes
of your back legs.
I tell people about this
but they don't care to stop
to admire
your inner iridescence,
this gold-rose flash of almost-wings
beside your head,
part sun, part blood.

There's a halo around you
where light catches
the fine fins of fur
that run along
the sides of your neck.
You are a noble-being
dressed in a high-collared dark cloak.
The V-shaped band of gray
that slips across
your white shoulders and chest
seems to hold the cloak in place,
clasped with a knot of bone.

Your shadowy polished eyes,

like amber crystals,
offer their light back to the world
in a casual blessing,
only a dog's glance,
while the spirit in you
sparks and swells,
a great tide expanding
from a single point.
This vibration touches me
until I have to turn away.

Puppy
Justin Chin

The best part of a man and a dog
Is the muzzle then the paw.

In the muzzle, find mercy.
In the paw, find comfort.

The best dog in my life ended sadly:
Bowzer was put down
When his muzzle got too grey,
His legs too arthritic,
And his mind too muddled:
He wouldn't notice cars
Backing out of driveways anymore;
Our favors fell to the cat.

In cartoons, the feline and the canine
Live as archetypical enemies, foils for comic plots;

But between your dog and my cat,
Our step-children, we call them,
We find things to believe in,
Things to cross that divide of genetics
And evolution, evidence.

How you touch my cat with your rough fingers and
Take her to drink out of the faucet.

How your dog panics and howls
Like a cow at the abatoir
When you go running in the park
Leaving him with me.
With his head on my lap,
We commiserate in our panic as we
Watch you slip out of our sight.

Mercy is falling asleep
In front of the telly
On a humid suburban California night
With the dog at our feet
The fleas biting,
Your mouth on my neck.
Is sleeping on my hard futon,
Our bodies twisted into shapes
That would disgust a chiropractor
So the cat can curl at blanket's edge.

This is what our animals tell me:

My passion for you is puppy strong
A gardenia floating in a dog's bowl.

Night Pee

Adrian Oktenberg

Your house seems so empty without you in it,
but when I find the key and enter
the rooms are warm, as if they have retained
your body and the breath of animals moving
through them. The dogs greet me with hallelujahs
of barking and dog-brouhaha, approaching
and backing off and coming, each wriggling
her polar bear head against my thigh.

I have come to walk them—delayed in town,
you called to sweetly ask this favor.
I don't mind when you ask like that.
Two feet of snow on the ground,
no traffic on the road, and branches creak above us.
Otherwise the night is silent, and stars shimmer
satellite greetings in faint colors.
I stand in misery, hating this cold, curse
my forgotten gloves, but the dogs don't mind.
They wear their heavy coats and no boots, and they ignore me,
busy tracing out whatever's so interesting
under the snow.

Dot stops, sniffs, digs fast with her paw,
but I'll never know what she finds there. When
at last Emma pauses and casually drops her hips
to pee, meanwhile looking around

in case any morsel of chipmunk should appear,
I feel grateful. She turns and runs the long
plowed driveway with such exuberance and speed
it forces me to murmur a brief salute. I feel my face crack
when I move my mouth to speak. My voice
sounds loud against the branches of stars and trees.
Sure enough, in a minute, like clock-work, Dot
pees too, and together they crowd up against the door
like riders rushing to board. I have to lean far out over them
to open it, worried I might slip and fall
on someone on the icy steps. Each takes up
a station on a different rug as I walk around
the rooms, turning on lights for you,
tuning the radio to jazz for them, warming at last.
I tell them you'll be back quite soon, all's well.
Tomorrow is New Year's Eve,
summer and all its smells will be upon us soon.

Courtly Love
Honor Moore

A rainbow, where it ends a red MG,
Texas plates, a friend's white empty kitchen.
Out the window a blond stick stretches
blue legs against a red barn door.
I can't see sweat, but her face is red,
hair flaxen, chopped blunt as if a mixing
bowl guided the scissor. Conversation?
Call it awkward. She had run ten miles.

Blood drenches the screen. Lear's sons conspire
on a green mountain. Woman. Knife. More
blood. After, from the car, the moon's slight
scythe doubles in the lake. She wears green
suede boots, speaks an English accent. We are
silent as we drive the length of a night
silver lake. Thank you, she says. I watch her
cross the dark lot, alight the red MG.

She bakes a cake on top of the wood stove.
The power has blown. It is a birthday
of mine. She sits in tweed, smoking, argues
down my bad love affair. Freak early snow
douses zinnias. She brings her border
collie, black and white. I spice hot cider.
She doesn't drink either. I always serve
spaghetti, ignorant she prefers beef.

She doesn't harangue when I call early.
She tells me a story from her life, paints
blue diamonds across my floor, dog thumping
its tail. The story is about fainting,
a painting, her encounter with a saint.
She asks me to read aloud. Her name means
fate. We drive to her new blue Fox. There is
tenderness in the force of her argument.

I have eye surgery and she cuts
lemons for chicken. In separate chairs
we watch a video about deaf love.
When I drag back from New Orleans, love
lost, she does not argue. The night I drive
north bearing soup through an ice storm, a sleigh
bed rocks at the edge of a frozen lake.
The dog licks my toes. She kisses first.

Red Parade
David Trinidad

Depressed because my
book wasn't nominated
for a gay award,

I lie on the couch
watching—not listening to—
the O.J. trial.

Byron, who senses
something's wrong, hides under the
bed until Ira

comes home, carrying
a bouquet of beautifully
wrapped tulips. I press

the mute button. "*This*
is your prize," he says. "Guess what
they're called." A smile in-

voluntarily
overcomes my frown. "What?" "Red
Parade." "That sounds like

the name of an old
Barbie outfit," I say. "That's
exactly what I

told the florist. And
you know what she told me?" "What?"
"When she was a girl,

she turned her Barbie
into Cleopatra: gave
her an Egyptian

haircut and painted
her nipples blue." "How cool." "Yeah,
but now she thinks that

her doll would be worth
eight hundred dollars if she
hadn't messed it up."

Once in water, the
tulips begin to unclench—
ten angry fists. Their

colors are fierce, like
Plath's "great African cat," her
"bowl of red blooms." Poor

Sylvia, who so
desperately wanted awards,
and only won them

after she was dead.
Byron jumps up, Ira sits
down and massages

my feet. "You guys." My
spirits are lifted by their
tulips, kisses, licks.

Blue Poodle
Jeffery Conway

3:10 A.M., I can't sleep. Heat some milk, pour it into a mug—
the one with the multi-colored poodles painted on it.
I'm staring at the blue one. Whoever heard of a blue poodle?
I saw a photograph of Doris Day in an L.A. museum once.
She had five or six poodles on leashes
and each dog was dyed a different color:
pink, green, yellow, and (now that I think of it) blue.
I have to pee, but there's no one to meet me halfway
between the bathroom and bed the way he did one night
last week. I flushed, started back through the dark
kitchen and there he was, nude, in the doorjamb—
arms braced on the frame, shivering. "Kiss me," he said.
I did, over and over, and held him for a long time.
The radiator clanked and gurgled in the otherwise
noiseless apartment. He was trembling, squeezed me tight.
I whispered into his right ear, "What's this all about?"
He said he didn't know, but I think we both know.
It's why I'm awake at this hour clutching this cup
of hot milk, afraid to walk to the bathroom
without him here. I fear moments like these
when his absence rushes at me like the steam that escapes
from this milk, the tiniest droplets
on the side of the mug forming the blue poodle's tears.

from "Atlantis"
Mark Doty

1. FAITH

       "I've been having these
awful dreams, each a little different,
though the core's the same—

we're walking in a field,
Wally and Arden and I, a stretch of grass
with a highway running beside it,

or a path in the woods that opens
onto a road. Everything's fine,
then the dog sprints ahead of us,

excited; we're calling but
he's racing down a scent and doesn't hear us,
and that's when he goes

onto the highway. I don't want to describe it.
Sometimes it's brutal and over,
and others he's struck and takes off

so we don't know where he is
or how bad. This wakes me
every night now, and I stay awake;

I'm afraid if I sleep I'll go back
into the dream. It's been six months,
almost exactly, since the doctor wrote

not even a real word
but an acronym, a vacant
four-letter cipher

that draws meanings into itself,
reconstitutes the world.
We tried to say it was just

a word; we tried to admit
it had power and thus to nullify it
by means of our acknowledgment.

I know the current wisdom:
bright hope, the power of wishing you're well.
He's just so tired, though nothing

shows in any tests, Nothing,
the doctor says, detectable;
the doctor doesn't hear what I do,

that trickling, steadily rising nothing
that makes him sleep all day,
vanish into fever's tranced afternoons,

and I swear sometimes
when I put my head to his chest
I can hear the virus humming

like a refrigerator.
Which is what makes me think
you can take your positive attitude

and go straight to hell.
We don't have a future,
we have a dog.
               Who is he?

Soul without speech,
sheer, tireless faith,
he is that-which-goes-forward,

black muzzle, black paws,
scouting what's ahead;
he is where we'll be hit first,

he's the part of us
that's going to get it.
I'm hardly awake on our morning walk

—always just me and Arden now—
and sometimes I am still
in the thrall of the dream,

which is why, when he took a step onto Commercial
before I'd looked both ways,
I screamed his name and grabbed his collar.

And there I was on my knees,

both arms around his neck
and nothing coming,

and when I looked into that bewildered face
I realized I didn't know what it was
I was shouting at,

I didn't know who I was trying to protect."

6. NEW DOG

Jimi and Tony
can't keep Dino,
their cocker spaniel;
Tony's too sick,
the daily walks
more pressure
than pleasure,
one more obligation
that can't be met.

And though we already
have a dog, Wally
wants to adopt,
wants something small
and golden to sleep
next to him and
lick his face.
He's paralyzed now
from the waist down,

45

whatever's ruining him
moving upward, and
we don't know
how much longer
he'll be able to pet
a dog. How many men
want another attachment,
just as they're
leaving the world?

Wally sits up nights
and says, *I'd like*
some lizards, a talking bird,
some fish. A little rat.
So after I drive
to Jimi and Tony's
in the Village and they
meet me at the door and say,
We can't go through with it,

we can't give up our dog,
I drive to the shelter
—just to look—and there
is Beau: bounding and
practically boundless,
one brass concatenation
of tongue and tail,
unmediated energy,
too big, wild,

perfect. He not only
licks Wally's face
but bathes every
irreplaceable inch
of his head, and though
Wally can no longer
feed himself he can lift
his hand, and bring it
to rest on the rough gilt

flanks when they are,
for a moment, still.
I have never seen a touch
so deliberate.
It isn't about grasping;
the hand itself seems
almost blurred now,
softened, though
tentative only

because so much will
must be summoned,
such attention brought
to the work—which is all
he is now, this gesture
toward the restless splendor,
the unruly, the golden,
the animal, the new.

Korean Mums
James Schuyler

beside me in this garden
are huge and daisy-like
(why not? are not
oxeye daisies a chrysanthemum?),
shrubby and thick-stalked,
the leaves pointing up
the stems from which
the flowers burst in
sunbursts. I love
this garden in all its moods,
even under its winter coat
of salt hay, or now,
in October, more than
half gone over: here
a rose, there a clump
of aconite. This morning
one of the dogs killed
a barn owl. Bob saw
it happen, tried to
intervene. The airedale
snapped its neck and left
it lying. Now the bird
lies buried by an apple
tree. Last evening
from the table we saw
the owl, huge in the dusk,
circling the field

on owl-silent wings.
The first one ever seen
here: now it's gone,
a dream you just remember.

The dogs are barking. In
the studio music plays
and Bob and Darragh paint.
I sit scribbling in a little
notebook at a garden table,
too hot in a heavy shirt
in the mid-October sun
into which Korean mums
all face. There is a
dull book with me,
an apple core, cigarettes,
an ashtray. Behind me
the rue I gave Bob
flourishes. Light on leaves,
so much to see, and
all I really see is that
owl, its bulk troubling
the twilight. I'll
soon forget it: what
is there I have not forgot?
Or one day will forget:
this garden, the breeze
in stillness, even
the words, Korean mums.

from *Paris France*
Gertrude Stein

And so France cannot change it can always have its fashions but it cannot change. And this brings me to dogs.

The french dogs which are native are useful dogs beautiful dogs but dogs that work. They are shepherd dogs and hunting dogs.

It is funny about dogs. Dogs resemble the nation which creates them at least we suppose so. Dogs are certainly like the people that own them and have them with them all the time. I like the word pastime as the french use it, it sounds so like the English word and yet the french make it so completely their own, who had it first this I do not know, but they certainly use it perhaps best. Dogs which are not useful dogs are a pastime, as one woman once said to me, one has a great deal of pleasure out of dogs because one can spoil them as one cannot spoil one's children. If the children are spoiled, one's future is spoilt but dogs one can spoil without any thought of the future and that is a great pleasure.

So the french dogs which are useful are native, the various shepherd dogs and the various hunting dogs, they are beautiful and they are useful, they are companions but they are not pets, they cannot be spoiled with pleasure to the spoiler as dogs that are pets can be spoiled, beside the useful animal is never a thing which is in or out of fashion, I always like the story of the shepherd near Aix-en-Provence, he was taking his dog to kill him he used to kill them by hanging, when they are eight years old they are no longer interested themselves in sheep, and as bread is dear you cannot keep a dog who is not interested in his trade. They know that at eight years of age he will stop being interested in tending sheep and so with tears streaming from his eyes off he goes to hang him. There is another nice story of a dog in Aix-en-Provence, there was a girl in a café who was very fond of a dog who used to come there regularly with a man and she regularly gave him a lump of sugar, one day the man came in without the dog and said the dog was dead. The girl had the lump of sugar in her hand and when she heard the dog was dead tears came to her eyes and she ate the lump of sugar.

The french have to have as pet dogs foreign ones which they change and fashion in their own way, and the mode in these dogs changes, they mostly always come back again, as long as I have known France first it was the poodles then it was Belgian griffons, fox-terriers, always called a fox, when I first heard it called a fox I thought it was a fox until I saw it, then Alsatian wolf hounds and Pekinese and then wire-haired terriers and now poodles, they have invented a new way to shave the poodle and a new color to make the poodles, so they are in again and this time at the same time the fox terriers have come back. Now all these dogs being of no use can be made fashionable, because fashion must never be useful, must very often be exotic, and must always be made to be french. That is what fashion is and it must change.

And this brings me back once more to the question of the resemblance of a dog to its country people.

It is a puzzle why are german dogs all rather timid gentle friendly and obedient, they are that, the characteristic german dogs, it kind of cheers one up that some time they the people will be that because people and dogs must be alike in a country in which they are born and bred and have descended. There are the poodles, the dachshunds, even the dog which is a kind of bull, a Bismark dog is gentle and the german black police-dog is a much gentler animal than the Alsatian wolf hound, it is a funny thing this, being fond of poodles, and always having them I bother about all this.

I thought poodles were french but the french breed always has to be refreshed by the german one, and the german pincher is so much more gentle than our Chichuachua little dog which it resembles, and so everything would be a puzzle if it were not certain that logic is right, and is stronger than the will of man. We will see.

Hyena
Jan Freeman

The hyena has a happy heart:
hearts, hearts, many hearts.
The hyena has a happy heart.
At noon she seeks them,
at dusk she finds them,
at night she grabs them, bleeds them, eats them.
The hyena grins at the scent of a lame one,
one in mourning, one in pain, one barely breathing:
weak ones! weak ones!
Sometimes they fold themselves
into her jaws;
mama, they cry.
She swallows the flesh.
She loves the blood, the silky gestures and the scrub,
the matted hair, each forlorn whimper.
So what if the lions hate her.

Portrait of the Artist as Porge Buck
(in a prospect of mutts)
Carl Morse

—with curtsies to Gertrude Stein

Some are taking longer and some are learning to draw

whereas others take learning longer and still draw

but learning to draw is longer always

when the learning it is taking others

is longer than the learner limning only and not rightly

taking the time to draw

oh, never the languid pussy but the lingering dog drawn large.

Skuppy the Sailor Dog
Eileen Myles

I was just thinking about influential books in my life. Most of them were illustrated. I am thinking about one in particular, right now, unmootly titled *Skuppy the Sailor Dog.* The plot was, or is, a little vague. Skuppy was a wandering sort of dog. Sailed the seven seas, made cameo appearances in various spots, one of which comes to mind is Turkey. Skuppy is standing in a sort of Medina where he
purchases a pair of purple slippers with curled-up toes. How astonished I was at the thought of a dog inserting his paws in such shoes. Skuppy is never shown actually wearing the shoes.

They do appear in one scene in Skuppy's small mildly lit bunker. At this point in his life, it seems Skuppy is in ownership of his own small tug. He is lying on the lower bunk of a two-decker and is quite alone and somehow you feel he is alone on the entire boat, it is his boat.

Yet the lighting is all right. A single sailor's lantern hangs on the wall, a tawny cozy yellow sprays around the room in a warm twinkling. The purple shoes lie discreetly at the foot of his bunker, his striped sailor's shirt folded neatly on a single wooden chair.

He's asleep at this point, with an ever so slight smile coursing his mouth, more of a glow than a smile.

Having good dreams, other places, countries, infinite new shoes to buy and strange people to purchase from. It is night of course and the boat is softly at sea, moving on its own correct course. Storm-free and guided by Skuppy, smiling at his dreaming.

A True Story
Joe Brainard

When I was a child, a strange thing happened. Mother and I were sleeping upstairs. It was just getting daylight, when we were awakened by a noise downstairs. Someone walked from the kitchen to the bottom of the stairs, then stopped. We listened. Who was it? We lived a long way from neighbors. Once more it walked to the kitchen. Then slowly it turned and came toward the stairway again. My heart stood still! Had someone come to kill us? Mother slowly slipped out of bed and crept to the landing. I watched her face, expecting her to break out into a scream, as she said, "My goodness! We forgot to put the dog out."

Dog Bite
Wayne Koestenbaum

I was locking my apartment door, on the way
    To the theater, when I was bitten by a dog,
An ash-gray poodle. Death cannot come on Thursday,
    I thought; I was conscious of my blood, clogged,
Slow-moving; I raised my pants-leg, gray
    Speckled with white, like Formica (this was foreplay

To the revelation) and saw the vampire circlet,
    The open hole the beast's mouth had made, my skin
Gashed. The poodle whimpered. It wore a bracelet
    Around its innocent neck. I ate grilled chicken
After the show, and a warm duck salad, and Chicklets
    In the car to heal my breath. I did not sicken

Until the morning. By the time I woke at ten
    A tidal wave had washed my consciousness
Far into the Pacific, past Hawaii, off Japan.
    I called my doctor, who said my recent tetanus
Booster protected me. But I felt as if some hymen
    I didn't know I possessed, powerless

And feminine, had been torn. Harley
    Was the dog's name: after the motorcycle?
I knocked on the owner's door. Was I acting queerly,
    Wishing to speak to her before my blood trickled
To a dead, dry halt? Jo Ann peered out. "I'm fairly

Ill myself," she said, "Your infection's local

And can't explain your dizziness. No dog
    Bite alone could make you queasy. I'm a dancer,
I'm always dizzy." I called her vet—I wanted dialogue
    With a professional—but there was no answer
In Buffalo, where Harley'd suffered shots in the fog
    Of his dog-consciousness. I called my friend Spencer,

Who worked three years in a rabies research lab.
    He said, "It's epidemic in New Jersey—five times
The normal incidence." I was imitating Job:
    Not budging, not complaining, letting God's crimes
Pile up. The bite, no longer raw, had formed a scab:
    "A scab!" cried Spencer (he looked like Jimmy Sims,

Lead singer in my third grade imitation
    Monkees rock band). He said, "This is serious.
Why are you being so lax?" I felt the strangulation
    That facts, paid too much court, impose: gangrenous
Accuracy. But Spencer understands my situation.
    He is gay, married (as it were), and not promiscuous.

So I followed his advice—I took my bite as law,
    A voice to be heeded. My mother, too, was bit
By a dog—owned by the Parvus, a family dark as Esau,
    And lawless. Mrs. Parvu kept their lawn uncut,
And her eldest son had been crippled, speeding at dawn,
    Drunk, on his motorcycle. He hadn't worn a helmet,

My parents pointed out. Parvu means: already seen?
    (Or is that *déjà vu*?) Their name has some relation
To vision, the future, or the past. I have been
    Terrified of the Parvus as of damnation:
Their motorcycles revving up, the boys' hair—duck's-ass,
        Brylcreemed—
    And their junky green refrigerator, a vision gleaned

Through their shadeless kitchen window. Mrs. Parvu
    Told my mother, "That dog doesn't bite.
You must have imagined it." Mrs. Parvu had a tattoo
    On her left shoulder. Under the weak streetlight
My mother couldn't find the wound, so back to her barbecue
    Went Mrs. Parvu (an anti-Semite,

We claimed), and my mother called the Health Department,
    Who put the Parvu dog in quarantine.
Thus, it seemed logical to seek my mother's judgment:
    Her words would soothe like powerful Bactine.
She'd survived her dog bite siege, and she is prescient
    About disease: she can read between its lines.

But she didn't answer her phone. Was it negligence?
    Was she out with her new man friend, Jim?
Sympathy, like Mercurochrome, rouged her countenance
    When, as a child, I fell off my Jungle Gym.
Was it more than a mere coincidence
    That my mother and I felt the venom

Of dog spit—dogs lunging at our right calves—

So close in time, when we'd feared bites for years?
When I reached her, she agreed to call her shrink on my behalf—
    To ask about my bite, not about being queer.
Dr. Fry said, "Just give good wound care." The scarf
    A fifties' mother wears when, on the pier,

A sea wind blows, and she wishes to protect her hair—
    A scarf with designs of Paris boulevards:
Well, I wrapped myself around my wound with the care
    That such a woman wraps her scarf, its colors tired,
Around her else-uncovered self. I had a nightmare
    Soon after my mother, walking past the yard

Of the Parvus (a stroll she takes each night
    To lower her blood pressure), heard their dog yap
And felt its teeth, the sharpened, hungry opposites
    Of Sandy's, her childhood dog. My dream: in the gap
Between my mother's life and mine I swam, a floodlight
    Revealing my bad breaststroke and my jockstrap—

I'd left my suit at home. Where's home? In the pool
    Of the emotions that we hold in common—
Our common blood—I dogpaddled. Implausible
    But true, before me yawned the golden canyon
Of Pavarotti's voice—and, moved by each syllable
    He sang, I felt his fine spittle, a poison,

Descend: manna, acid rain. Is my mother's genius
    A venom that makes me foam?
New York is rabies-free, but poison is a Proteus,

It changes form: the furniture of her home
Is fanged. I am stepping now within the radius
    Of the wet kiss Kurt's mother gave—her dome

Of bouffant hair a kind of synagogue
    To me when I slept over at Kurt's house—
Or the wet kiss, waking me, of Kurt's dog—
    Or the patch of sidewalk I feared, zone of Gladys,
Three houses down, a mutt-haunted faubourg
    ("Gladys"—the name—sounded to me like "lettuce"):

When I braved her porch, my presence set off chimes
    (The chain of red glass squares, a hex that hung
Inhospitably above my head), and her seraphim,
    Five chihuahuas, raced to the screen and sang
A bark version of *Carmina Burana.* I was first stung
    In the company of my mother's delphiniums:

Aloof from my friends, poised on my Sting-Ray's
    Kickstand balanced on our driveway, transfixed
By a game of TV-tag, I felt my bike give way
    And I fell into the flowers. The acoustics
Of the block were acute: my mother, playing hooky
    Across the street, came running, and, allergic

Herself to much of life, she drove me to a specialist
    For shots. I used to bite myself: I paved
The way for Harley. When I got mad, I could resist
    Violence to others by gnawing my own finger. Laved
By my spit, marked by my teeth, I could say—I exist.

I bite, therefore I am. My finger is still chafed

Where I, for years, have ravaged it—a scratching post,
    A philosopher's stone: animal and human minds
Require a surface to rub against, a host
    For their own incubus. My teeth always find—
As a witch finds her familiar, a widow her ghost
    Husband in Hades—the chewed-on spot, signed

By previous bitings: a place I have not lost.
    I'm glad I never called the Health Department
On Harley: I'm still breathing, and the Boy Scouts
    Taught me to live in fear of those omniscient
Beasts that know the art of reading human thoughts
    Through the ill-concealing walls of an apartment.

A goldfish tossed in a garbage can—a good
    Fish-friend for a week—haunts me as if it were a poet.
My second pet, a turtle, died of dryness. It was my étude
    In life, and I botched the exercise. I forgot
To dispense its daily tablespoon of food,
    And the water grew green and still with thick brine clots.

My sister, in puberty, picked up a stray,
    Without my mother's consent, and named it "Tish."
We kept it in the garage, and got it spayed.
    I always felt poignant when I gazed at its dish
Of mess, but I would turn from pity, go in to play
    My Bach. That dog bite week, my plants perished

From the heat, and I wore shorts, without a bandaid
    To cover the wound. That way, when people asked
To see the bite, I could blazon it, like a newlywed
    Proud of her ring. My bite, after all, is an odalisque—
Nude, reclining, aloof, and staring straight ahead
    Into the future, like a fitted death mask:

When I even think about the bite, I get an ache
    Above my stomach, as if I can't digest
The memory of the dog, wandering in the wake
    Of a carnival down a dusty road, on an overcast
Thursday in the Veneto (I think of Proust's Balbec,
    The sea-town where he longs for girls, for the conquest

Of time): we asked, in a town whose name I can't recall,
    For directions to the *cimitero*—a cemetery
Celebrated for the tomb of the Brionvega family.
    (We didn't know this yet, but our friend Bill
Had died that week of AIDS.) No one in the carnival
    Procession understood our question. A collie—

I am guessing, I have never cared to know the names
    Of the various dogs—trailed behind the cars
And carts and bicycles, and having searched in vain,
    We thought, for the cemetery—was it hidden in that far
Mass of trees?—we took our eyes from the road, and cries of pain
    Two seconds in the future almost struck our ears

With what we had not done, but nearly done:
    The dog—collie? Saint Bernard?—limped offstage,

Old and gray. We'd almost hit it. A woman in cretonne
Shook her finger at us in a feint of rage.
Was it her dog? Then we found our Brionvega tomb,
And signed the guest book, and visited the graves.

Dead Dog
Dennis Cooper

The children want to bury the
body in our rose garden beside
their fortress, and they want a
young oak to plant upon it where
they will build a tree house
named after him, Abbey—king of
one year of their lives. He was
their drunkenness and drugs, the
blind spot in their eyes, running
in from the bus stop calling his
name until he would lose his mind.
Now they lug him, fall down, shriek
because he got as close to their
mouths as a kiss, then give up,
leave him halfway there and run off,
their hands clawing the television,
stereo, hungry to fill up their
wild lives. Not with a dead
dog but with something great.

Giacometti's Dog
Robin Becker

She moves so gracefully on her bronze legs
that they form the letter *M* beneath her.
There is nothing more beautiful than the effort
in her outstretched neck, the simplicity of the head;
but she will never curl again in the comfortable basket,
she will never be duped by the fireplace and the fire.

Though she has sniffed out cocaine in the Newark Airport,
we can never trust her good nose again.
She'll kill a chicken in her master's yard,
she'll corner a lamb in the back pasture.
She's resigning her post with the Seeing Eye.

Giacometti's *Dog* will not ask for water
though she's been tied to a rope in Naples
for three days under the hot sun.
Giacometti's *Dog* will not see a vet
though someone kicks her and her liver fills with blood.
Though she's fed meat laced with strychnine.
Though her mouth fills with porcupine quills.

Giacometti's *Dog* is coming back
as a jackal, snapping at the wheels
of your bicycle, following behind in her
you-can't-touch-me-now suit.
Giacometti's *Dog* has already forgotten

when she lost the use of her back legs
and cried at the top of the stairs
and you took pity on her.

She's taking a modern-day attitude.
She knows it's a shoot-or-get-shot situation.
She's not your doggie-in-the-window.
She's not racing into a burning house or taking your shirt
between her teeth and swimming to the beach.
She's looking out for Number One,
she's doing the dog paddle and making it
to shore in this dog-eat-dog world.

I wasn't cruising him I was
Gavin Geoffrey Dillard

I wasn't cruising him I was
cruising his dog

When he stopped to be stroked my
hands rejoiced

He was big and blond and had a
delicate waist

His master was handsome too

On Bleaching My Hair
Gerry Gomez Pearlberg

I don't talk much about my sex life &
there's more to that than you'd think.
More than mystery.
More than the desire to maintain a private stance.
It's certainly not a question of shyness.
Of that, I can assure you.

I've always wanted to bleach my hair.
Actually, it first occurred to me recently,
the week I turned thirty.
I say I've always wanted to bleach my hair
because it sounds so much more
like something someone blond would say.

I thought being blond might help me
assume a new identity. It has.
My head is a prop.
Impressive things are going on behind the scenes.
The stage lights are off, but the curtain is up.

People ask if it's true about blondes having more fun.
I say, "More fun than what?"

Bleach makes you look like an artificial martian.
This, to many people, is frightening.
To many of these same people it is also a turn-on.

These individuals comprise my target audience.
By the way, it only works if you're not *naturally* blond.
Preferably, you're a brunette like me.
Only someone who's been dark all her life
has the sense of irony to properly carry blondeness off.
Blondeness to the fullest extent of the law.

Speaking of which, I've started carrying a switchblade.
This has certainly made walking my dog more exciting.

On the subject of dogs:
they help you meet women.
I'm only interested in girls
who are interested in dogs,
but it's much easier to get women
who don't have dogs
to sleep over at your house.
The ones with dogs are always running off to feed them.
Often, they will remember to do so
just prior to or immediately following sex.
Frequently, it preoccupies them throughout
the sex act, rendering it perfunctory.

Deviant sex, I deeply believe, should *never* be perfunctory.

Nonetheless, sadly,
I have been on both ends of this phenomenon
on more than one occasion.
The trick, I've learned,
is to find women who *love* dogs

& perhaps *want* dogs,
but don't actually *have* dogs.
When you yourself have a dog, these women will find you.

This is otherwise known as moving the mountain to Mohammed,
& its implications, like those of blondeness, are vast.

Gay Dogs
Jack Anderson

These dogs must be gay.
Straights don't act that way.
Straights behave,
Mind their manners, know their place.

But these dogs keep circling,
Padding, prowling, running in packs,
They keep sniffing and licking
One another in public.

Can you imagine? In public!
Such shameless displays!
O naughty gay dogs!
You ought to be spanked!

For Holly
Eloise Klein Healy

Holly look at that old dog it puts its gray face
under a hand and Holly I swear I am that dog.

Look at me wiggling here at your side your wise eyes
must know you are my friend and now here comes
my old gray face again and my nose nudges
all afternoon at your hand.

I would shed all over you Holly if it would mean
you would carry me around with you for a day wearing
the colors of my coat without concern for brushing
and plucking and cleaning away the hairs.

See I will uncurl here on the floor and sleep
on my side an old dog and faithful friend
who stays where you can reach me near your feet
and ready to move when you move.

This has to do with our lives Holly and not at all with our poems.

The Dog
Melinda Goodman

Come on   come on
she calls the dog
to the open car door
till the shaggy black
and white excitement
jumps wagging into the back
pushing his head
through the gap between the seats
brown eyes shining
through his bangs at her
like kindergarteners peeking
through the curtain
of their first school play

He licks his nose
she turns the key
backing full speed
down the driveway
and they're off
her silver hair glistens
his toenails dig
in the leather seat
in her rearview mirror
she sees him watching
dogs fly by
her eyes on the road

fingers wrapping the wheel
till mile after mile   finally
a dead end
the perfect stop
she pulls to the curb

and lets him out
he sniffs   he pees   he shits
she lights a cigarette
he runs here   runs there
the soft crew cuts of tended lawns
feels good on his toes
he runs smiling up to some children
following their ball
one to the other
they call him monkey
in the middle
back and forth
till glancing back
through silly eyes
he sees her car gone
with him just a shaggy spot
on her rearview mirror
her midnight metallic blue
disappearing into broad daylight

racing madly after
her blue smoke
he passes
tree tops   dump trucks   malls

tearing down the road
his tongue like a flag
for miles his bangs blow back
his ears are rags
to the horns and screeches
catching her at an intersection
her door flies open
and slams him inside
he smiles at her with bloody feet
as she drives them
home

Scroppo's Dog
May Swenson

In the early morning, past the shut houses,
past the harbor shut in fog, I walk free and
single. It is summer—that's lucky. The whole
day is mine. At the end of our village I stop
to greet Scroppo's dog, whose chain is wrapped
around a large dusty boulder. His black coat
is gray, from crouching every day in the gravel
of Scroppo's yard—a yard by a scrap-filled pond,
where Scroppo deals in wrecked cars and car parts.
I guess he gets them from crashes on the expressway,
or from abandoned junks he loots by the roadside.

I don't know the name of Scroppo's dog. I remember
him, years ago, as a big fierce-looking pup.
It may have been his first day chained there,
or shortly after, that he first greeted me:
his eyes big nuggets shooting orange sparks, his
red tongue rippling out between clean fangs—
fangs as white as lilies of the valley that bloom
in a leafy border by Scroppo's weathered porch.
It was late May, as now, when with sudden joyful
bark, black fur erect and gleaming, the dog
rushed toward me—but was stopped by his chain,
a chain then bright and new. I would have met
and stroked him, but didn't dare get near him,
in his strangled frenzy—in his unbelief—

that something at his throat cut short
his coming, going, leaping, circling, running—
something he couldn't bite through, tripped him:
he could go only so far: to the trash in the weeds
at the end of the driveway, to the edge
of the oily, broken cement in back, where Scroppo's
muddy flatbed truck stands at night.

Now, as I walk toward him, the dog growls,
then cowers back. He is old and fat and dirty,
and his eyes spit equal hate and fear.
He knows exactly how far he can strain
from the rock and the wrapped chain. There's
a trench in a circle in the oily dirt his paws
have dug. Days and weeks and months and years
of summer heat and winter cold have been survived
within the radius of that chain.
Scroppo's dog knows me, and wants to come and
touch. At the same time, his duty to expel
the intruder makes him bare his teeth and
bristle. He pounds his matted tail, he snarls
while cringing, alternately stretches toward me
and springs back. His bark, husky and cracked,
follows me for a block, until I turn the corner,
crossing the boundary of the cove.

I've never touched Scroppo's dog, and his
yearning tongue has never licked me. Yet, we
know each other well. Subject to the seasons'
extremes, confined to the limits of our yard,

early fettered by an obscure master in whose
power we bask, bones grow frail while steel
thickens; while rock fattens, passions and
senses pale. Scroppo's dog sniffs dust.
He sleeps a lot. My nose grows blunt, I need
to remember the salty damp of the air's taste
on summer mornings, first snowfall's freshness,
the smoke of burning leaves. Each midday,
when the firehouse whistle blows, a duet
of keen, weird howls is heard, as, at the steep
edge of hopelessness, with muzzle pointed,
ears flat, eyes shut, Scroppo's dog forlornly
yodels in time to the village siren sounding noon.

Requiem
Terry Wolverton

It is a sunny winter morning and I am struggling with you
to carry—up your steep hillside—the frozen body
of your dog.

Your first dog, Pencil, the good dog, the lady.
Who would sit with her front paws crossed, so dainty.
Who was often seen with a dog food can stuck on the end
    of her nose.
Who would press her face against your thigh and rest there
for as long as you let her.

Sunday she was playing with young girls in the laundromat.
Today she is dead and frozen like a popsicle and we are
trying to avoid your landlord as we trudge upward
with her stiff heavy carcass.

You tell me, "Pencil is still with me, but you are gone."
I don't feel gone, with this cold weight in my arms.
I have held you all night long, trying to make myself
more real to you than death. We have been failing
for a long time.

We at last reach the top, lower her body to the dirt.
You will spend the day digging. I advise you to let the other dogs
see her, so they will stop searching for her.

You disconnect your phone. Days pass. Though I hear you screaming at me in my dreams, I do not return to your hillside where Pencil lies deep in the earth.

In Dreams You Come to Me
Fran Winant

There are dark lines around your eyes,
drawn as if to accent your beauty.
In dreams, you come to me
as a woman I have just met.
We love each other at first sight.
The white of your dog-chest
has become a white blouse.
The black of your dog-back
has become a black suit.
You have long, dark human hair now,
swept around your head,
arms instead of paws.
We're the same height now,
just as we are when you dog-leap
onto my chest,
and we're mouth to mouth,
as we have often been.
More comfortable to embrace
now that we're both the same species.
There's electricity between us.
Our closeness must be expressed
quickly,
before the dream ends
and we resume our usual places,
I at my desk,
you on the floor.

rant
Jules Mann

I think when I saw the baby westheimer terrier prancing through the immensely tall grass in the park is when it hit because nikki was there for all of our life together before things turned bad—he was this ethereal little creature   you'd   only   had   for   three   days   when   we decided to live together he was your plaything and your nemesis always scampering up to you or wriggling out of reach and when I decided to move out almost two years later you took him back up to the property where you got him, left him in a cage nearby with a note tacked on it saying "I can't take care of this dog anymore my wife is dying of cancer and he just reminds me too much of her"—this was about three months after you tested positive and I was getting on with life while yours must have stood terribly still as you went through every routine without telling anyone you never even told me and we were married michael we were practically fucking married even though we're both gay we traveled to europe together slept in the same bed our dinner parties were famous and now you've gone and died on me and we never made our peace

Virgil's Villanelle

Timothy Gerken

for Robert

You told me to lie on my bed on the floor
then left me for eight days.
Though to me it seemed longer.

In circles I turned and turned
searching for a way
to lie on my bed on the floor,

and keep an eye on the door.
When John came we walked and played
for hours, though it seemed longer.

I knew you hadn't gone to the store,
but for an endless hospital stay
while I waited for you on the floor.

Each time the elevator door
opened, I'd bark and bay
hoping that it wouldn't be any longer,

that you'd be home before
the end of the day,
and we'd be in your bed off the floor.

We'd lie together with my paw
on your chest and stay
until morning, though it would seem longer.

When you came home just a little stronger
and I nosed and rubbed my favorite odor
you lay down on my bed on the floor
for an hour, though to me it seemed longer.

Canis Major
Aleida Rodríguez

As far as we're concerned, she is the best
Jack Russell terrier that ever lived.
At such a claim, you'll wink, "Boy, they're *obsessed!*"

But she is scary-smart and, we profess,
the most streamlined specimen of her breed.
With hula hoops we've proved she is the best

acrobatic jumper—and, you might guess,
we'd have to give her high marks on her glib
rebarks. We know, you'll say we are obsessed.

Yet we know, too, you would be most impressed
by how she snarls at dogs who're thrice as big
as she. Just to be fair, she is the best

at night, below the covers, at her rest:
We call her Baby Jesus in His Crib.
Alright, alright, so what if we're obsessed

with her three spots lined up with such finesse
and whorls of hair that form a curly bib?
Our inner dog tells us she is the best,
even if you think us terrier-obsessed.

a dog's poem
Kitty Tsui

for Rompkof's Migette O'Woodside,
a.k.a. Meggie Tsui, Senior

it was a nightmare that time
i broke out
of a dog-proof (woof, woof!) house
when my newly-adopted mom
left to go on tour.

i panicked,
thought she had left me
so i broke free,
determined to bring
her home.

at first i gladly scavenged
barbecue bones at Flint's.
but soon
i lost my appetite for everything
but to find my mom.

days and night merged.
sun, moon, stars,
i ran and ran and ran
strangers all around,
cars speeding past.

lost in an alien place,
asphalt, tar, exhaust,
no familiar smells.
i ran and ran and ran
till my pads were torn and bloody.

i ran and ran and ran till
a woman called to me
one hot afternoon.
she had a soft, kind voice
but she was not my mom.

suddenly two dogs ran out.
i was afraid
but they sniffed me and smiled.
the woman put out water
so i drank.

then i caught
the sound of
a Volkswagen engine
and a familiar smell—
my mom!

i leapt on her but
she had fallen to her knees.
i covered her wet face with kisses,
shouting:
my mom, my mom, my mom!

Lucky
Melanie Hope

I was never the kind of bitch
That took much shit
Not when I had a say in it
That is

My first stop on this journey
Was a big mistake
They cut my tail and left me
For someone else to take

But my story has a very good end
I was taken home by two lesbians

—Boonji

Little Prayer to the Big Goddess
James Broughton

I dreamed I was
your little black spaniel
I wagged you
and woofed you
everywhere
I led you with my leash
licked your hand
leapt in your lap
slept on your bed
lived for your pats

You were the best master
any doggie ever had
You taught me
astounding tricks
so I would be known as
Big Joy Mother's
bright little bowwow
the most adoring
follower of the Divine
in the canine world

O Great Mother of
Beast and Biped
let me be your
permanent panting pet
drooling with
dogged devotion

Dog
Linda Smukler

All I smell is dog and all I know is dog   all I care for is heart and mouth
all I see is fine soft and head beneath my nails   fine   please and thanks
all I know is dog   big and lovely   herd of gazelle   through the brush I see
a pond full of concentric and not so concentric circles for issue and stick
all I know is pond now summer and yellow swim and raspberries off the vine
the back seat of any car far and formal and the reissue of mud   all I know
is god and toe and the stick in one hand frisbee in the other thrown so far
I cannot make it out in the grass   all I know is dog   collared and streak in
play in come in solid weight on my lap in absolute confidence and exhaus-
tion from squirrel chase all I know is dog   Liv Ullman eyes   sweet like
flan

from "Dangerous Memory"
Judith McDaniel

I.

My body knew the sound of a gun
before my brain. From the floor
of the boat where I had already
thrown myself, I thought,
that was a gunshot and was afraid.

Running this morning along the bank
of the Hudson I remembered

walking single file along the edge
of the Rio San Juan, not knowing
where I was being taken, strung out
along a jungle path as men
with guns told us where to walk
and how fast.
                    I remembered the Hudson then,
remembered jogging one day with my dog
and how at the end of the run she had decided
she wasn't done running and slipped away
to play. As I searched along the riverbank
the sun was setting and dark was rising
from the dark river water. What I
had planned for myself—a run, then dinner
and a quiet evening—were no longer mine

to plan and the river seemed to whisper
give up, you can't control this now
as I searched and wept and cursed the dark
gathering along that riverbank.

And in the August heat, as a man
motioned me along with his rifle
I could hear the same whisper
you can't control this now
and felt myself grow numb as the sunlight
filtered through the jungle leaves
that whispered *surrender* in my ear.

I found my dog in pieces on the highway
later that night and wept and raged and mourned.
You loved her because of what she was
a friend reminded me. She loved to be free.
Her death was in
how she was in life
and if you loved her life
don't you have to love her death? I did
and wondered as I walked
through that jungle who would love
my death who would understand
what brought me down this jungle path.

Saints
Mark Bibbins

When I look at Benson it's impossible
for me not to see you. I think he knows this.
No one had the nerve, when you asked us for a
puppy, to say no;

by that time, the KS had spread to your lungs
and the doctors had cut your calendar from
months to weeks. You just wanted to die at home,
so we moved you there.

Any one of us would have been happy to
take Benson after you were gone, but I had
the yard, and you insisted. On the day we
brought him to you, I

remember hoping we could have him paper-
trained by the time he came to live with me, not
because I couldn't cope with pee on my rugs—
I just didn't know

how else to measure your time. Nobody can
explain what happened, though, when the two of you
met. We were worried the dog might start chewing
on your IV tube

or something, but he just put his ebony
head on your chest and closed his eyes. After you

stroked him for a few minutes, you smiled and fell
into a deep sleep.

When you woke up, something had changed. You started
eating (constantly) and even your breathing
improved. Benson terrorized the rest of us,
chewing up our shoes,

the usual puppy antics, but with you
he was always calm and gentle. The doctors
were perplexed by your improvement, but it made
perfect sense to us.

Today I was at the Cloisters, staring at
an image of Saint Roch hanging on a cool
granite wall. When he was twenty he made a
pilgrimage to Rome,

where he cured victims of plague and cholera
by making the sign of the cross over them.
But he too fell ill and dragged himself into
a forest to die.

This was where Roch was found by a dog who licked
his sores, fed and nursed him until he was well.
The dog remains at his side in the peaceful
gloom of the Cloisters.

You died, not after a few weeks, but two years,
and now, each day, Benson wakes me with sloppy
kisses that say *Get up—let's go outside.* And
they say *Remember.*

Dogs
Eliza Galaher

Big ass
Gap pants
rich
expensive pup
Gotta smoke?
Don't smoke
Don't smoke?
Gotta
black dog
and you won't
give me a smoke?
What kinda shit is that!
Gotta
black dog
and she won't give
me a smoke!
What a racist, man
What a fuckin' racist!
He's right he's right
and I pull my leash
a little tighter.

Expert
Jennifer Willoughby

The nights don't hurt her anymore.
Before, the tight subsonic cramp
squeezed her closed, the way a prizefighter,
awakening years after the final round,
suddenly can't clench his fist
without wincing, without pain.

She's been lucky—
she's gained the trust of animals.
Dogs empathize with drive-by fucks,
with tender sleaze, the human right
to interchange capillary lust
with the honest need to run.

An expert told her greyhounds make poor pets.
At night, alone, they get a lupine urge
to start racing over rivers, roads, and parks
until they can't find home, lost and quivering
but with a new, feral sense of heart.

It took her years to get over a bad idea.
But as in running, the comfort
of the motion worked with time.
The lunge line slacked and frayed.
She said "*rapture*" and began.

Old Yeller Wall Paper
Gerry Gomez Pearlberg

Like that good old dog
they had to shoot
there are different ways
of carving up
the heart's dead weight:
chronology, trauma, deceit,
and burnt umber grief
linger like lockets
you lost the key to,
still chained
around your neck.

Sometimes, no matter
how wrong it might be,
it just feels too good
to stop.
Today's the kind of day
you'd take a dog out
to be shot,
foaming at the mouth.

Fear's like wall paper,
hue upon peeling hue:
velvet ivy borders,
floral stains,
nose-diving dogs.
Underneath the underneath

inky glue is smeared
along four walls
that cradle and confine.
The soul's thin halls
are membrane keyholes
you can listen
through. Many
layers, many hues.

Steam the heart open
like an envelope.
It's all floral disasters, ivy
chokers and
dirt hounds
salivating for some
abstract bone
a million miles
from home.

Layers of paper
line the walls of rooms
you used to live through.

Wishful thinking
is a room that does
not fit inside itself,
floors akimbo, windows
overblown. Desire's in
the doghouse of the heart
gnawing its paw.

It's no different
across town:
there the heart is also,
and also there.
Across the blue ocean,
it crosses the street
without holding your hand.
It foams at the mouth,
and is nothing more
than motor pulse,
voluntary and
involuntary spasms
set off by bright electro-
lytes: yeah,
sometimes
the hard facts
soothe us,
other times they're
like a yellow dog
dragged by its collar
out back
behind the shed,
called out back
by love, rubbed
on the ear
by the ambidextrous
thumb of love

then shot,
real quick,
dead on.

Porcupine
Jan Freeman

If I write blue yellow green

or you wish the floors down so the house is open as a window

If a tree stump feeds the birds or the fish sleep till spring

the frogs drowse in muddy beds and stones shine with frost

the cascading branches above the field the mountains stacked behind the
    goats—

When the morning sings now and the dogs on the scent of
    the porcupine

foolishly drag you through the woods thrilled with the thought

of conquest and all along you can't stop them though you know it's pain
    and poison

around another bend and you keep running as if your company

will save them though you might have simply stopped and tied each one
    around a tree

and made them feel something more than thrill—perhaps a red squirrel
    or a flock of turkeys

or even a chipmunk would turn their heads to safety

but on and through you go as if you too need some proof that whatever
    tastes best kills fastest

and that old love sitting beside the beech tree tried to show you that three
    years ago—

Now it's all loss and fabric and time mending—it's perpetual task—time
    stacked like minutes or weeks or years

even as we wait to pull love's quills out, anesthetized by our own foolish
    disappointment—

all along the chase was ill-fated—you couldn't stop your hands from flying
    and legs from stretching

and your eyes still look for that sign even as your skin begs for reprieve
    and you wonder if you
let it all go will you simply starve to death or lose the ability to feel any-
    thing beyond the flat despair
and loss grins and grins from the branches of the tallest trees,
    multiplying
as you catch the curves and there in the midst of those tilting mouths
is the porcupine fat and bending a branch thirty feet up—waiting as you
wait to see if the dogs finally barking hysterically can leave what
they've spent the days tracking—as she sits ominous as a thick down draft
or a sharp light reflecting some piece of storm in the middle of the sky—
Who will rescue you if you can't turn back? Who will take the time—
the barbs spread beneath the skin—to pull and pull and your mouth still
    healing from the last scramble
when you left everything and then twisting the predicted ending lost it all
    for passion
and it was so routine—
Here you have the chance to break away but still the dogs throw themselves
against the trunk and the low branches and the porcupine shifts her
    weight as you
pray she doesn't fall—knowing that once the spiral begins, descent cannot
    lift her head—
and hands are an avenue toward breaking once the sorrowful smile, the
    bushy exterior, lethal
reflects everyone and everything ever desired in your foolish and broken
    life.

My Dog Is Named for Elizabeth Bishop
Robyn Selman

October. The first pricks of cold air in
the city morning. We walk, Liz and I,
up then down in the same uneven line.

Her ears as sharp as sharpened pencils,
she pulls me along her wayward travels.
She darts out headlong, paces ahead,

coming and going and leaving again,
the way shadows seem to meet the tops of heads,
dissolve and are newly elongated.

We like the early, early morning best.
Our view is, thankfully, how we left it.
Nothing has stirred yet, the news lies unread.

Except for the weather, it's all so still,
and no one is walking out of our world.

Knowing
David Levinson

His body graces my bed, asleep.
Muscles under skin relax in the
cool dry luxury of my air conditioner.
He's not been out all day long, trained
he is to the sound of my keys in the door.
Still, he does not pick up his canine
head, does not shift on the firm, square
mattress and sheet that has become
his bed for months now. His smell lingers
in the hallway, the elevator—an earthy
perfume, pungent, mine. I scratch behind
his ears, trail a finger across the soft
lips of his muzzle. He does not budge,
lost in dog-eared sleep. This I know
of him. My bulldog. He likes long walks
on the beach, a bath on Sunday, scraps
for dinner. And sometimes, a kiss in
the morning after coming home
from roaming the neighborhood. The
spoiled smell of another on his lips.

On the Phone
Chrystos

you whisper in a soft
country drawl
I wanna be
your natural pussy hound
Wanna lick the moon
between your thighs
till my tongue is silver full
Give it to me now
I need
you to burn for me
Wanna hear you gasp
That's right honey
give me some
of your sweet stars
Fly for me howling
down to a hungry dog
ass in the air
I wanna take you
till there's nothing
left but satisfied

for Denise

Side Show
Gerard Wozek

Jimmy played the Dog-Faced Boy
he wagged and foamed
behind steel bars at the circus
his unclipped nails, hairy arms and face
provided him with gainful employment
but public ridicule
for years we'd bring milkbones
to the circus
and watch him chew them with relish
gawkers would often tease him
throw spit balls or
crumpled sacks with peanut shells in them

I sometimes dreamt of Jimmy's escape
dreamt of his warm dog man body
dreamt his tail between my legs
his tongue in my ears
his teeth in my skin—just hard enough

One night I snuck out to unlock his cage
found Jimmy curled in a corner
studied his heavy breathing
touched his neck
felt my pulse rise
felt myself harden
then the dog eyes opened

his nostrils flared with my scent
our instincts began to meld

Jimmy on all fours
Jimmy my Dog-Faced Boy
Jimmy my Master

Using the Poet's Bathroom
Lawrence Schimel

for R.H.

The Greeks were only half correct
that a woman might turn men's flesh hard as stone;
    yours, perhaps, would not grow erect

at the sight of her, but of her own she has
    complete control. Looking inward,
so like mirrors' truths, Maude, too, turned stone: topaz

    gems that floated in her bladder.
You tell this tale to explain why, like a male
    dog, she lifts one leg to splatter

the black plastic bags of garbage with her scent,
    a splendid anecdote about
your discovery that she was a latent

    hermaphrodite. But there is more
at stake than regaling friends on midnight walks
    with Maude, who had waited hours

for your return without an accident. Such
    is the devotion of women
and dogs; the strength of will to endure so much

        time alone, sustained only by
the idea of your commitment to them. Maude
        held tight to her purpose. The gay

man's best friend, it was not in imitative
        flattery she tried to grow a
penis, but because she recognized your love

        of sameness over difference.
A threshold she could not fully cross, her attempts
        at genital enlargements

contradicted your earlier lines: *a choice*
        that always, when there is a door,
even a French one, must be made. Sacrifice

        her identity, though she tried,
Maude was left whining about sex and her
        crepuscular gender, outside

your bathroom door. In that earlier poem,
        Max, too, whined; for both dogs *the word*
toilet clearly suggests twilight, some

        subliminal ending. They were
restricted to those parlors overflowing
        with your public life, books and art:

needlepoint pugs on pillows, porcelain pugs,
        pugs in every medium, all gifts.

Pigs, too, for they had monopolized your thoughts

    before your vowels lengthened. On
an island all of vowels, Odysseus
    had come to know and love swine.

Returned to Ithaca, his sole *memento*
    amori was a piggy bank—
two copulating corpulent pigs into

    whose empty bellies he dropped coins
for his son's wedding. Only his faithful dog,
    after sniffing at the man's loins,

had recognized him. Though too short to reach
    men's crotches, Maude could smell where your
true affections lay. In your bathroom, where flesh

    is exposed from its civilized
garb, ostensibly free from all onlookers
    except that narcissean gaze,

there is no room for animals. Photographs
    of men cover every surface
(the ceiling even!) as if this were a hive,

    each man locked into his own frame
like a cell of memory's honey, and when
    the shower fills the room with steam

these boys, unlike bees, do not flee. Mentors, friends,
    lovers, the men who have shaped your life,
it was yet too soon to know if I would stand

    among their ranks. I stood before
their ancient glittering eyes and unzipped my
    pants. I could not hope to compare.

Dog in a Manger
Michael Lassell

Rest in peace, little bowser, perfect pup
companion of an unidyllic up-
bringing. You were the toy-fetching face-and-
foot-licking love of a fat boy so sand-
bagged for affection you could have called him
anorexic. Dad bought you on a whim—
seeing I wasn't any good at ball
games. You yelped hello, gave a wag, ate all
the Nativity set angels. Caio, my
impish confidant, elfin friend. Good-bye.

There was, of course, no dog. Mama's I.D.
was spic-and-span impeccability.
I got a bird in its own cage instead.
And, by the way, my mother too is dead.

Lament for Toby, A French Poodle
May Sarton

The great Toby is dead,
Courteous and discreet,
He of the noble head,
Remote and tragic air,
He of the trim black feet—
He's gone. He is nowhere.

Yet famous in New Hampshire
As one who fought and killed—
Dog-bane and dog-despair—
That prey that all resign,
The terrible and quilled,
Heraldic porcupine.

He will become a legend,
Black coat and royal nature,
So wounded he was blind,
As on a painted shield
Some lost heroic creature
Who fought and would not yield.

If we were brave as he,
Who'd ask to be wise?
We shall remember Toby:
When human courage fails,
Be dogged in just cause
As he before the quills.

Growing Dark
James Schuyler

The grass shakes.
Smoke streaks, no,
cloud strokes.
The dogs are fed.
Their licenses
clank on pottery.
The phone rings.
And is answered.
The pond path
is washed-out grass
between green
winter cover.
Last night in
bed I read.
You came to
my room and
said, "Isn't
the world
terrible?" "My
dear..." I
said. It could be
and has been
worse. So
beautiful and
things keep getting
in between. When

I was young I
hurt others. Now,
others have hurt
me. In the night
I thought I heard
a dog bark.
Racking sobs.
Poor guy. Yet,
I got my sleep.

The Irony of the Leash
Eileen Myles

Life is a plot to make me move.
I fill its forms, an unwitting
                          crayon

          I am prey to the materials
of me, combinations
          create me into something
   else, civilization's inventions

numb me, placate me
              carry me around. I
am no better than a dog.
  My terms are not bark
              and howl

but I often get drunk and rau-
cous, often I need to get
laid so bad I imagine my
howls lighting up the neighborhood
              pasting rings
          around the moon.

As a child I was very in love
with the stars. As a human
    a victim of my perceptions
it is natural that I should love

light and as a passive dreamer

it is natural I should be attracted
to the most distant inaccessible
light. What do you make of
this. Friend? I need the reass-
                              urance

of human voices so I live with
a phone or I go out and seek
my friends. Now they are always
different, these people who
happen to be moved by the same
            music as me, whose
faces I like, good voices,

I can recognize the oncoming footsteps
of a person I like. In this
I am little better than a dog.

Sometimes I go to movies and I
sit in the dark. Leaving the light
and relishing the movements
            of images occurring
         in another time, bright
and pretty, sometimes gruesome

and violent and though I know
very well,

        (as I paid my 1.50 and came

in here and chose a seat
        a decision based on the condition
of my eyesight and my place
    in society
I may sit in the front or
the back, am I old,
        am I young...)

I know very well that this movie is not
    real, yet I am often
in the grips of fears more real
than those my own life throws up
for my unwilling complicity

and I am visibly shaken, often
        nearly screaming with fright
and revulsion...

                    yet I know it is not real.

Movies have caused me to become
an artist. I guess I simply
        believe that life is not
    enough. I spin dreams
of the quotidian out of words I
could not help but choose.

They reflect my educational background,
    the economic situation of
        my parents and the countries

their parents came from. My words
            are also chemical reflections:

metabolically I am either fast or
            slow, like short words or
            long ones, sometimes I
like words which clank hard against
    each other like a line of
                wooden trains. Sometimes
I wish my words would meld
to a single glowing plastic tube slightly
    defying time.   I write
quite a bit,

            I no longer believe in religion
but find writing an admirable
                substitute,
I don't particularly believe in art
but I know that unless there is
    something I do which is
at least as artificial and snide
                and self-perpetuating...

well then I would have to find
someone else who
            had that sort of handle
on things and hold onto him
        for dear life.

I would be less than a dog.

I think it's important to have
    your own grip on
  things, however
that works and then you should
pursue that and spend the
       rest of the time
doing the ordinary.

Exactly like a dog. Dogs
are friendly creatures unless
    they've been mistreated.
They like to eat and run around.
They neither drink nor smoke
nor take drugs. They are perfect.
         They mate freely
whenever they have the urge.
They piss and shit according to
their needs, often they appear
to be smiling but of course
they are always happy.
Interestingly enough,
it is quite popular, particularly
in the city in which I live,
to own a dog, to walk him on a
             leash
morning noon and night, people with
families have dogs and they add
      to the general abundant chaos
   of the household,

people who live alone own dogs. For
protection, regularity and
the general sense of owning a friend.
People love their dogs and undoubtedly
their dogs love them. Though
they are faithless and impersonal.
They love their owners because
they feed them, stroke them,
bring them outside to run around if a dog gets injured
its owner will take it to a doctor or
a clinic, depending on the economic
        situation of the owner.

Dogs do not believe in God or Art.
Intrinsically they have a grip
            on things.

I unfortunately do not. I sit
here with a bottle of beer, a cigarette
            and my latest poem, *The Irony of the Leash*.

August 6

Now and Again: An Autobiography of Basket
Angie Estes

for Gertrude Stein

Comets are like scythes, they do not hold
your coat, although they may look
as if they are going to, just rounding
the corner into the century, but perhaps she was
speaking of commas, celestial bodies trailing
bright hair every seventy some years,
once through a lifetime if you're lucky
you see them, two women and a poodle
curved into hummocks, asleep
and slung between sheets, still now
and again her mouth would open,
grin, and then bear down
on something it looked like dahlias
she carried in her teeth and time
and time again it was my name,
so sometimes we danced, my paws
on her shoulders in the garden of Bilignin
while she sang *I am I because my little dog
knows me* to the tune of "On the Trail
of the Lonesome Pine," *each part needing its own
place to make its own balancing*
as in a sentence she said, there is a mirror
of that and another photo, too,
where we sit as we were told to

on the sofa in front of the portrait
she painted me on the wall behind, when time
and time again she told me to sit
because she loves me in that painting
she says there I am God's dog, ASCOB,
who barks all the time but is impossible
to hear, that *my* epitaph, too, should declare
Any Solid Color Other than Black
when the time comes to call
everything back to where it belongs,
to its place in some long sentence
where I was going to say we are
the commas, tipped like hammocks
in the wind, but then again now
I think, rather, we are the hammocks
in which the commas swing.

Identity A Poem
Gertrude Stein

PLAY I

I am I because my little dog knows me. The figure wanders on alone.

The little dog does not appear because if it did then there would be nothing to fear.

It is not known that anybody who is anybody is not alone and if alone then how can the dog be there and if the little dog is not there is it alone. The little dog is not alone because no little dog could be alone. If it were alone it would not be there.

So then the play has to be like this.

The person and the dog are there and the dog is there and the person is there and where oh where is their identity, is the identity there anyway.

I say two dogs but say a dog and a dog.

The human mind.   The human mind does play.

The human mind.   Plays because it plays.

Human Nature. Does not play because it does not play again.

It might desire something but it does not play again.

And so to make excitement and not nervousness into a play.

And then to make a play with just the human mind.

Let us try.

To make a play with human nature and not anything of the human mind.

Pivoines smell like magnolias

Dogs smell like dogs

Men smell like men

And gardens smell differently at different seasons of the year.

PLAY 2

Try a play again
Every little play helps
Another play.

There is any difference between resting and waiting.
  Does a little dog rest.
  Does a little dog wait.
  What does the human mind do.
  What does human nature do.

A PLAY.

  There is no in between in a play.
  A play could just as well only mean two.
  Then it could do
  It could really have to do.

The dog.   What could it do.

The human mind.   The human mind too.

Human nature. Human nature does not have it to do.
  What can a dog do and with waiting too.
  Yes there is when you have not been told when to cry.
  Nobody knows what the human mind is when they are drunk.
  Everybody who has a grandfather has had a great grandfather and that
great grandfather has had a father. This actually is true of a grandmother
who was a granddaughter and grandfather had a father.
  Any dog too.
  Any time anyone who knows how to write can write to any brother.
  Not a dog too.
  A dog does not write too.

ANOTHER PLAY

But. But is a place where they can cease to distress her.

ANOTHER PLAY

It does not make any difference what happens to anybody if it does not make a difference what happens to them.

This no dog can say.

Not any dog can say not ever when he is at play.

And so dogs and human nature have no identity.

It is extraordinary that when you are acquainted with a whole family you can forget about them.

ANOTHER PLAY

A man coming.

Yes there is a great deal of use in a man coming but will he come at all if he does come will he come here.

How do you like it if he comes and look like that. Not at all later. Well anyway he does come and if he likes it he will come again.

Later when another man comes

He does not come.

Girls coming. There is no use in girls coming.

Well anyway he does come and if he likes it he will come again.

PART IV

The question of identity.

A PLAY.

I am I because my little dog knows me.
Which is he.
No which is he.
Say it with tears, no which is he.
I am I why.
So there.
I am I where.

ACT I SCENE III

I am I because my little dog knows me.

ACT I SCENE

Now this is the way I had played that play.
But not at all not as one is one.

ACT I SCENE I

Which one is there I am I or another one.

Who is one and one or one is one.

I like a play of acting so and so and a dog my dog is any one of not one.

But we in America are not displaced by a dog oh no no not at all not at all at all displaced by a dog.

SCENE I

A dog chokes over a ball because it is a ball that choked any one.

PART I   SCENE I

He has forgotten that he has been choked by a ball no not forgotten because this one the same one is not the one that can choke any one.

SCENE I   ACT I

I am I because my little dog knows me, but perhaps he does not and if he did I would not be I. Oh no oh no.

ACT I   SCENE I

When a dog is young he seems to be a very intelligent one.

But later well later the dog is older.

And so the dog roams around he knows the one he knows but does that make any difference.

A play is exactly like that.

Chorus   There is no left or right without remembering.

And remembering.

They say there is no left and right without remembering.

Chorus   But there is no remembering the human mind.

Tears   There is no chorus in the human mind.

The land is flat from on high and when they wander.

Chorus   Nobody who has a dog forgets him. They may leave
                him behind. Oh yes they may leave him behind.

Chorus   There is no memory in the human mind.

And the result

May be and the result

If I am I then my little dog knows me.

The dog listens while they prepare food.

Food might be connected by the human mind but it is not.

SCENE II

And how do you like what you are
And how are you what you are
And has this to do with the human mind.
Chorus   And has this to do with the human mind.
Chorus   And is human nature not at all interesting. It is not.

SCENE II

I am I because my little dog knows me.
Chorus   That does not prove anything about you it only proves
                  something about the dog.
Chorus   Of course nobody can be interested in human nature.
Chorus   Nobody is.
Chorus   Nobody is interested in human nature.
Chorus   Not even a dog
Chorus   It has nothing to do human nature has nothing to do
                  with anything.
Chorus   No not with a dog.
Tears   No not with a dog.
Chorus   I am I because my little dog knows
Chorus   Yes there I told you human nature is not at all
                  interesting.

SCENE III

And the human mind.
Chorus   And the human mind
Tears   And the human mind
Chorus   Yes and the human mind.
   Of course the human mind

Has that anything to do with I am I because my little dog knows me.
What is the chorus.

Chorus   What is the chorus.

Anyway there is the question of identity.

What is the use of being a little boy if you are to grow up to be a man.

Chorus   No the dog is not the chorus.

SCENE II

Any scene may be scene II

Chorus   And act II

No any act can be act one and two.

SCENE II

I am I because my little dog knows me even if the little dog is a big one and yet a little dog knowing me does not really make me be I no not really because after all being I I am I has really nothing to do with the little dog knowing me, he is my audience, but an audience never does prove to you that you are you.

And does a little dog making a noise make the same noise.

He can almost say the b in bow wow.

I have not been mistaken.

Chorus   Some kinds of things not and some kinds of things.

SCENE I

I am I yes sir I am I.
I am I yes madame am I I.
When I am I am I I.
And my little dog is not the same thing as I am I.
Chorus   Oh is it.
With tears in my eyes oh is it.
And there we have the whole thing
Am I I.
And if I am I because my little dog knows me am I I.
Yes sir am I I.
The dog answers without asking because the dog is the answer to anything
that is that dog.
But not I.
Without tears but not I.

ACT I   SCENE I

The necessity of ending is not the necessity of beginning.
Chorus   How finely that is said.

SCENE II

An end of a play is not the end of a day.

SCENE IV

After giving.

Talking to Dogs
W. H. Auden

In memoriam Rolfi Strobl. Run over, June 9th, 1970

From us, of course, you want gristly bones
and to be led through exciting odorscapes
  —their colors don't matter—with the chance
of a rabbit to chase or of meeting
  a fellow arse-hole to snuzzle at,
but your deepest fury is to be accepted
  as junior members of a Salon
suaver in taste and manners than a pack,
  to be scratched on the belly and talked to.
Probably, you only hear vowels and then only if
  uttered with lyrical emphasis,
so we cannot tell you a story, even
  when it is true, nor drily dissect
in the third person neighbors who are not there
  or things which can't blush. And what do we,
those of us who are householders, not shepherds
  or killers or polar explorers,
ask from you? The admiration of creatures
  to whom mirrors mean nothing, who never
false your expression and so remind us
  that we as well are still social retards,
who have never learned to command our feelings
  and don't want to, really. Some great men,
Goethe and Lear, for instance, have disliked you,

132

which seems eccentric, but good people,
if they keep one, have good dogs. (The reverse
          is not so, for some very bad hats
handle you very well.) It's those who crave
          a querulous permanent baby,
or a little detachable penis,
          who can, and often do, debase you.
Humor and joy to your thinking are one,
          so that you laugh with your whole body,
and nothing dismays you more than the noise
          of our local superior titters.
(But then our young males are dismayed by yours
          to whom, except when a bitch is air-borne,
chastity seems to present no problem.)
          Being quicker to sense unhappiness
without having to be told the dreary
          details or who is to blame, in dark hours
your silence may be of more help than many
          two-legged comforters. In citizens
obedience is not always a virtue,
          but yours need not make us uneasy
because, though child-like, you are complete, no New
          Generation whom it's our duty
to disappoint since, until they notice
          our failings, they will never bother
to make their own mistakes. Let difference
          remain our bond, yes, and the one trait
both have in common, a sense of theatre.

Contributors

Jack Anderson is a dance critic for *The New York Times* and the author of eight books of poetry. His poetry has appeared in various anthologies, including *The Name of Love: Classic Gay Love Poems* and *The Party Train: A Collection of North American Prose Poetry*.

W. H. Auden (1907-1973), widely considered to be the first authentically modern poet writing in English, wrote numerous books, opera libretti and plays, including "The Dog Beneath the Skin."

Robin Becker's most recent poetry collection is *All-American Girl*.

Mark Bibbins lives in New York City, where he studies poetry at The New School. His poems have appeared in other anthologies and journals including *The Paris Review* and *The James White Review*.

Joe Brainard (1941-1994) was a visual artist and writer whose drawings, collages and paintings are in the collections of the Museum of Modern Art and the Whitney Museum, among others. He also published numerous books during his lifetime. A new edition of *I Remember* was published by Penguin Books in 1994.

Since 1948, **James Broughton** has produced many works of poetry and poetic film. His most recent publications include *Special Deliveries* (collected poems), *The Androgyne Journal* (a prose confession), *Making Light of It* (a poetics of cinema) and *Coming Unbuttoned* (a memoir). His most recent film, *Scattered Remains,* was commissioned by the San Francisco Film Festival in 1988.

Ana Marie Castañon's work appears in two recent anthologies, *My Lover Is a Woman: Contemporary Lesbian Love Poems* and *The Zenith of Desire,* as well as in the journals *The Evergreen Chronicles* and *Sinister Wisdom.*

Justin Chin is a writer and performance artist. He is the author of *Bite Hard.* He lives in San Francisco.

Chrystos is a Native American writer and political activist whose poetry is widely acclaimed. Her books include *Fire Power* (1995), *Fugitive Colors* (1995) and *In Her I Am* (1993).

Jeffery Conway is the author of *Blood Poisoning*. His work has appeared in many magazines and anthologies, including *Plush* and *Eros in Boystown: Contemporary Gay Poems about Sex.*

Bernard Cooper's most recent book is *Truth Serum.* He received the 1991 Earnest Hemingway Award and a 1995 O. Henry Prize. His work appears in *The Best American Essays of 1998,* as well as in several anthologies of gay literature.

Dennis Cooper is the author of the novels *Guide, Try, Frisk* and *Closer,* the graphic novel *Horror Hospital Unplugged,* and *The Dream Police: Selected Poems: 69-93.*

John Del Peschio's work has appeared in the magazine *Art Today.* He lives in Brooklyn Heights and often walks by an old wood building listed in an 1847 City of Brooklyn directory as a men's hairdressing parlor. He likes to think Walt Whitman went there.

Gavin Geoffrey Dillard is the author of numerous books, the editor of *Between the Cracks: The Daedalus Anthology of Kinky Verse,* a photographer, artist, songwriter for Disney and self-described "cat person."

Tim Dlugos' writing has appeared in *Best American Poetry, The Paris Review, Poets for Life, Christopher Street* and *BOMB.* He was the author of several volumes of poetry. He died of AIDS in 1990 at the age of forty. *Powerless: Selected Poems 1973-1990* by Tim Dlugos was issued posthumously by High Risk Books in 1996.

Mark Doty is the author of four collections of poetry, including *My Alexandria* and *Atlantis,* and a memoir, *Heaven's Coast.* He is the recipient of numerous awards for his work, including a Whiting Writer's Award, and grants from the NEA and the Guggenheim Foundation.

Angie Estes, author of *The Uses of Passion,* was the winner of the 1994 Peregrine Smith Poetry Competition. She is an Associate Professor of English at Cal Poly, San Luis Obispo, and has published critical articles on Louisa May Alcott and Margaret Wise Brown.

Edward Field's *Counting Myself Lucky: New and Selected Poems 1963-1992* won a Lambda Award. He collaborated with Neil Derrick on the novel *Village,* and also edited two books by the late Alfred Chester. His study of Fritz Peters appeared in *The Harvard Gay and Lesbian Review.*

Jan Freeman is the author of *Hyena* and *Autumn Sequence.* Her poems appear in numerous anthologies, including *The Oxford Anthology of Women Poets, The Arc of Love* and *The Zenith of Desire.* She is the director of Paris Press and lives in western Massachusetts with her sheepdogs, Dorothy Parker and Emma Goldman.

Eliza Galaher is a writer/performer whose work has appeared in *The New Fuck You: Adventures in Lesbian Reading* and *The Zenith of Desire.* She lives with her beloved dog, Amy.

Tim Gerken lives in New York City and teaches at CUNY's Medgar Evers College. He received his MFA from Brooklyn College in 1994. Regarding his poem, "Virgil's Villanelle," Tim writes: "Virgil is an Irish Retriever who lived with Robert Farber. I met Robert and Virgil at the Edward Albee Foundation in 1992. Robert died in December 1995."

Melinda Goodman teaches poetry workshops at Hunter College in New York City. Her poems have appeared in numerous lesbian magazines and anthologies in the U.S., Great Britain and France. *Middle Sister,* a collection of poems on growing up lesbian in America, was self-published in 1988.

Thom Gunn's books include *The Man with Night Sweats, Collected Poems* and a collection of essays, *Shelf Life.*

Richard Harteis' latest book of poetry, *Keeping Heart,* was published in a bilingual edition by Orpheus House in 1996 during a Fulbright year at the American University in Bulgaria. He has been awarded a fellowship to the Camargo Foundation in Cassis, Southern France where he will be living during the winter and spring of 1997.

Eloise Klein Healy is the Associate Editor of *The Lesbian Review of Books* and the chair of the MFA in Creative Writing Program at Antioch University Los Angeles. Her most recent collection of poetry, *Artemis in Echo Park,* is also available on CD/audio tape from New Alliance Records. She co-owns two Portuguese Water Dogs.

Melanie Hope is a poet who lives in New York City. Her work has appeared in *The Caribbean Writer, Sinister Wisdom, Essence, The Arc of Love* and *The Key To Everything.*

Michael Klein has a memoir out from Persea and two books of poems, *1990* and *Day and Paper* from Provincetown Arts Press. He teaches at Sarah Lawrence College and Goddard College in Vermont.

Wayne Koestenbaum is the author of two books of poems, *Ode to Anna Moffo and Other Poems, Rhapsodies of a Repeat Offender,* as well as two books of prose, *The Queen's Throat: Opera, Homosexuality, and the Mystery of Desire* and *Jackie Under My Skin: Interpretting an Icon.* He received a Whiting Writer's Award in 1994.

Michael Lassell is the author of *Poems for Lost and Un-Lost Boys, Decade Dance* and *The Hard Way.* He is the editor of *Eros in Boystown, The Name of Love* and (with Lawrence Schimel) *Two Hearts Desire.*

David Levinson is working on a novel, *A Gun in My Absence,* about a family in the deep south of Texas.

Timothy Liu's books of poems are *Vox Angelica* and *Burnt Offerings.* A new book, *Say Goodnight,* is forthcoming from Copper Canyon Press.

Jules Mann resides in San Francisco with her Golden Retriever, Gevrey. Her work appears in *Between the Cracks* and *The Zenith of Desire.* She is the author of two chapbooks, *Loud Nipples* and *Get Naked and....*

Judith McDaniel is a writer and activist. Her most recent book is *The Lesbian Couples Guide.*

Honor Moore's book of poems, *Memoir,* was published by Chicory Blue Press (1988). *The White Blackbird,* a biography of her painter grandmother, Margarett Sargent, was published in 1996 by Viking.

Carl Morse co-edited, with Joan Larkin, *Gay and Lesbian Poetry in Our Time,* and is the author of *The Curse of the Future Fairy,* the revenge oratorio *Impolite to My Butchers* and a book of plays, *Fruit of Your Loins.* His poems also appear in *Three New York Poets.*

Eileen Myles' books include *Maxfield Parrish: Early and New Poems* (1995) and a book of fiction, *Chelsea Girls,* both from Black Sparrow Press. With Liz Kotz, she edited *The New Fuck You: Adventures in Lesbian Reading,* which received a Lambda Book Award. Since 1990, she's shared her life with Rosie, a pit bull terrier.

Adrian Oktenberg won a Barbara Deming Fund grant for her collection of poems, *The Bosnia Elegies,* published by Paris Press in 1997. She is also a winner of the Astraea Foundation's Lesbian Writers Fund Award (1995). She lives in Northampton, MA. Her partner Jan Freeman's two sheepdogs are named Emma Goldman and Dorothy Parker.

Gerry Gomez Pearlberg is the editor of *The Key to Everything: Classic Lesbian Love Poems* and *The Zenith of Desire: Contemporary Lesbian Poems about Sex.* She edits an occasional 'zine called *DogStarGirl* and lives in Brooklyn with her boxer Otto.

Aleida Rodríguez, recipient of an NEA poetry fellowship, is the 1996 winner of *The Spoon*

River Poetry Review Editors' Prize, which also features five of her poems in its Spring 1997 special issue on gay/lesbian/bisexual poets. *ZYZZYVA* has commissioned an essay by her for their "Being and Becoming a Writer" series.

May Sarton (1912-1995), the Belgium-born American poet and novelist, authored numerous books including *Letters From Maine, The Silence Now: New and Uncollected Poems* and *Collected Poems 1930-1993.*

Lawrence Schimel is the editor of *Switch Hitters: Lesbians Write Gay Male Erotica and Gay Men Write Lesbian Erotica; Food for Life and Other Dish; Two Hearts Desire: Gay Couples on Their Love;* and is author of *Drag Queen of Elfland,* among other books.

James Schuyler (1923-1991) was a Pulitzer Prize-winning poet, novelist and playwright. His *Collected Poems* is available from Farrar, Straus, and Giroux.

Robyn Selman is the author of a poetry collection *Directions to My House.* Her poems have appeared in *Ploughshares, The Paris Review, The American Poetry Review* and numerous other publications.

Linda Smukler is the author of *Normal Sex* and *Home in Three Days. Don't Wash.*, with accompanying CD-ROM. She has received fellowships in poetry from the New York Foundation for the Arts and the Astraea Foundation. She is co-editor, with Susan Fox Rogers, of *Portraits of Love.*

Gertrude Stein (1874-1946) was an American poet, playwright, novelist and literary experimentalist. Her works include *Three Lives* (1909), *Tender Buttons* (1914) and *The Autobiography of Alice B. Toklas* (1933).

May Swenson (1919-1989) received numerous honors during her career as a poet, including Guggenheim and Rockefeller fellowships, and an Award in Literature from the National Institute of Arts and Letters.

David Trinidad is the author of several volumes of poetry, most recently *Answer Song.* He lives in New York City.

Kitty Tsui is the author of *Breathless* and *Sparks Fly,* written under the pseudonym Eric Norton. Her constant companion is Meggie Too, a vizsla.

Jennifer Willoughby is an MFA candidate at the University of Minnesota Creative Writing Program. She is the 1996 recipient of the Loft Gay and Lesbian Inroad Program Scholarship. Her work has appeared in *The James White Review, Nimrod, The Evergreen Chronicles, Sing Heavenly Muse* and elsewhere.

Fran Winant has received a NYFA poetry grant and an NEA painting fellowship. Her books are *Looking at Women, Dyke Jacket* and *Goddess of Lesbian Dreams.* Her poems have appeared in many anthologies, including *The Arc of Love* and *The Penguin Book of Homosexual Verse.* Her dog paintings have appeared in *The Sexual Perspective* and *Hammond's Lesbian Art.*

Terry Wolverton is the author of the novel *Bailey's Beads* and the poetry collection *Black Slip.* Another novel, *The Labrys Reunion,* will be published by New Victoria Publishers in 1997. Terry teaches creative writing and has edited several literary compilations, among them *His* and *Hers.*

Gerard Wozek's poems have appeared in various journals and anthologies, including *Backspace, Off the Rocks, Gents, Bad Boys and Barbarians* (1995) and *Reclaiming the Heartland* (1996). His first chapbook, *The Changeling's Exile,* was published in 1995. He lives in Chicago.

Eva Yaa Asantewaa, former dance critic and radio interviewer, is a psychic counselor and educator with roots in the Caribbean and in Spirit. She grew up around dogs but later came out as a cat devotee. She was a contributor to *The Zenith of Desire.*

Permissions

"Dogged Love" and "Gay Dogs" © 1997 by Jack Anderson. Used by permission of the author.

"Talking to Dogs" from *Collected Poems* by W.H. Auden, edited by Edward Mendelson © 1971 by W.H. Auden. Reprinted by permission of Random House, Inc. and Faber and Faber Ltd.

"Giacometti's Dog" from *Giacometti's Dog* by Robin Becker © 1990. Reprinted by permission of the University of Pittsburgh Press.

"Gay Dog" and "Saints" © 1997 by Mark Bibbins. Used by permission of the author.

"A True Story" by Joe Brainard reprinted from *New Work* © 1973 by permission of John Brainard, executor of the Estate of Joe Brainard.

"Little Prayer to the Big Goddess" © 1997 by James Broughton. Used by permission of the author.

"the same dogs" © 1997 by Ana Marie Castañon. Used by permission of the author.

"Puppy" © 1997 by Justin Chin. Used by permission of the author.

"On The Phone" © 1993 by Chrystos from *In Her I Am,* Press Gang Publishers, Vancouver, B.C. Reprinted by permission of the author.

"Blue Poodle" © 1991 by Jeffery Conway. First published in *B City,* Fall 1991. Reprinted by permission of the author.

"Pet Names" © 1995 by Bernard Cooper. First published in *Unleashed: Poems by Writers' Dogs,* Crown Books, 1995. Reprinted by permission of the author.

"Dead Dog" © 1979 by Dennis Cooper, from *Idols* by Dennis Cooper, The Seahorse Press. Reprinted in 1989 by Amethyst Press. Reprinted here by permission of the author.

"Fifi, the dangerous fag dog" © 1997 by John Del Peschio. Used by permission of the author.

"I wasn't cruising him..." © 1987 by Gavin Geoffrey Dillard from *Pagan Love Songs* by Gavin Geoffrey Dillard, Bhakti Books. Reprinted by permission of the author.